Childhood and Child Welfare in the Progressive Era

A Brief History with Documents

Related Titles in
THE BEDFORD SERIES IN HISTORY AND CULTURE
Advisory Editors: Natalie Zemon Davis, *Princeton University*
Ernest R. May, *Harvard University*
Lynn Hunt, *University of California, Los Angeles*
David W. Blight, *Yale University*

LOOKING BACKWARD: 2000–1887 *by Edward Bellamy*
Edited with an Introduction by Daniel H. Borus, *University of Rochester*

HOW THE OTHER HALF LIVES *by Jacob A. Riis*
Edited with an Introduction by David Leviatin

Muckraking: Three Landmark Articles
Edited with an Introduction by Ellen F. Fitzpatrick, *University of New Hampshire*

PLUNKITT OF TAMMANY HALL *by William O. Riordon*
Edited with an Introduction by Terrence J. McDonald, *University of Michigan*

THE JUNGLE *by Upton Sinclair*
Edited with an Introduction by Christopher Phelps, *The Ohio State University at Mansfield*

Talking Back to Civilization: Indian Voices from the Progressive Era
Edited with an Introduction by Frederick E. Hoxie, *University of Illinois at Urbana-Champaign*

TWENTY YEARS AT HULL-HOUSE *by Jane Addams*
Edited with an Introduction by Victoria Bissell Brown, *Grinnell College*

MULLER V. OREGON: *A Brief History with Documents*
Nancy Woloch, *Barnard College*

THE REBUILDING OF OLD COMMONWEALTHS *and Other Documents of Social Reform in the Progressive Era South*
Edited with an Introduction by William A. Link, *University of North Carolina at Greensboro*

The 1912 Election and the Power of Progressivism: A Brief History with Documents
Brett Flehinger, *California State University, San Bernardino*

OTHER PEOPLE'S MONEY AND HOW THE BANKERS USE IT *by Louis D. Brandeis*
Edited with an Introduction by Melvin I. Urofsky, *Virginia Commonwealth University*

THE BEDFORD SERIES IN HISTORY AND CULTURE

Childhood and Child Welfare in the Progressive Era

A Brief History with Documents

James Marten

Marquette University

BEDFORD/ST. MARTIN'S   Boston ♦ New York

*Dedicated to the staff of the Children in Urban America Project,
1999–2004*

For Bedford/St. Martin's

Executive Editor for History: Mary V. Dougherty
Director of Development for History: Jane Knetzger
Developmental Editor: Ann Hofstra Grogg
Editorial Assistant: Carina Schoenberger
Senior Production Supervisor: Joe Ford
Production Associate: Chris Gross
Senior Marketing Manager: Jenna Bookin Barry
Project Management: Books By Design, Inc.
Text Design: Claire Seng-Niemoeller
Indexer: Books By Design, Inc.
Cover Design: Billy Boardman
Cover Photo: Children Running as a Group along Cambridge Avenue, Chicago, Ill., 1911;
Photographer *Chicago Daily News.* DN-0057417. Courtesy Chicago Historical
Society.
Composition: Stratford Publishing Services
Printing and Binding: Haddon Craftsmen, an RR Donnelley & Sons Company

President: Joan E. Feinberg
Editorial Director: Denise B. Wydra
Director of Marketing: Karen Melton Soeltz
Director of Editing, Design, and Production: Marcia Cohen
Manager, Publishing Services: Emily Berleth

Library of Congress Control Number: 2004107797

Manufactured in the United States of America.

0   9   8   7   6   5
f   e   d   c   b   a

For information, write: Bedford/St. Martin's, 75 Arlington Street, Boston, MA 02116
(617-399-4000)

ISBN: 0-312-40421-2
EAN: 978-0-312-40421-5

Acknowledgments

Acknowledgments and copyrights appear at the back of the book on page 181, which
constitutes an extension of the copyright page.

Foreword

The Bedford Series in History and Culture is designed so that readers can study the past as historians do.

The historian's first task is finding the evidence. Documents, letters, memoirs, interviews, pictures, movies, novels, or poems can provide facts and clues. Then the historian questions and compares the sources. There is more to do than in a courtroom, for hearsay evidence is welcome, and the historian is usually looking for answers beyond act and motive. Different views of an event may be as important as a single verdict. How a story is told may yield as much information as what it says.

Along the way the historian seeks help from other historians and perhaps from specialists in other disciplines. Finally, it is time to write, to decide on an interpretation and how to arrange the evidence for readers.

Each book in this series contains an important historical document or group of documents, each document a witness from the past and open to interpretation in different ways. The documents are combined with some element of historical narrative—an introduction or a biographical essay, for example—that provides students with an analysis of the primary source material and important background information about the world in which it was produced.

Each book in the series focuses on a specific topic within a specific historical period. Each provides a basis for lively thought and discussion about several aspects of the topic and the historian's role. Each is short enough (and inexpensive enough) to be a reasonable one-week assignment in a college course. Whether as classroom or personal reading, each book in the series provides firsthand experience of the challenge—and fun—of discovering, recreating, and interpreting the past.

Natalie Zemon Davis
Ernest R. May
Lynn Hunt
David W. Blight

Preface

Much of what Americans love and hate about government originated during the Progressive Era, which lasted from roughly the mid-1890s through the First World War. From public health to criminal justice, from the regulation of commerce to the direct election of U.S. senators, from women's suffrage to the federal income tax, from the conservation of natural resources to the prohibition of alcohol, Progressive reforms introduced Americans to large-scale public and private efforts to shape the lives of ordinary Americans. These reforms marked an important shift in Americans' attitudes about personal and governmental responsibility, and were important precursors to the even greater expansion of government responsibilities and services in the 1930s and 1960s.

Childhood and Child Welfare in the Progressive Era focuses on Progressive activism as it related to children and youth. In the crucibles of the cities, where social problems facing children were magnified and obstacles often seemed insurmountable, Progressives tried out programs that have been imitated ever since. Many of the problems they attempted to solve continue to confront urban children today, especially in the areas of education and juvenile justice. Youngsters constitute a large percentage of Americans dependent in whole or in part on those federal, state, and local programs and institutions that are descended from Progressive Era child welfare reforms.

The documents in *Childhood and Child Welfare in the Progressive Era* manifest the contours of children's lives during a crucial period in American history. An introduction offers a brief history of the conditions facing children in America's cities, of evolving attitudes toward children, and of the rise of Progressive ideals as they related to child welfare reform, particularly in the fields of health, child labor, and juvenile justice. The documents that follow provide samples of Progressive discourse on the plight of city children and the methods proposed to help them. The final documents draw on the words of children and youth themselves, who show the fun as well as the peril in urban children's lives.

In this book, whenever possible, the experiences and points of view of African Americans and of girls are included, but the selections available are limited by Progressive Era attitudes about race and gender. Although African Americans—generally referred to as "colored" by whites and blacks alike early in the twentieth century—certainly appear in the following documents, the African American population was still overwhelmingly rural and southern, and, as a result, was generally ignored by Progressive Era researchers and reformers. In addition, because most observers believed the "boy problem" to be the greatest social crisis facing American cities, most research dealt with male children and youth rather than females.

A number of student aids accompany this brief history and the documents. Chapter introductions and document headnotes provide historic contexts and biographical information to help readers make sense of the featured reports, studies, and memoirs. A chronology of child welfare reforms in the Progressive Era situates many of the people, programs, and publications mentioned in the text in relation to larger developments. Questions for consideration offer possible avenues for papers and class discussion. The bibliography highlights the historiographies of Progressivism and children and youth.

ACKNOWLEDGMENTS

Many individuals contributed to this project. Michael Grossberg, Indiana University; Joseph E. Illick, San Francisco State University; David I. Macleod, Central Michigan University; Steven Mintz, University of Houston; and David S. Tanenhaus, University of Nevada, Las Vegas, provided helpful comments on the entire manuscript. At Bedford/ St. Martin's, David W. Blight and Patricia Rossi were encouraging, and Carina Schoenberger, Emily Berleth, and Jane Knetzger tended to important details. Ann Hofstra Grogg and Nancy Benjamin were extraordinary editors, helping me make sense out of sometimes conflicting readers' reports and offering enthusiastic, commonsense suggestions for strengthening the manuscript. David McDaniel, Barbara Fox, and Timothy McMahon also contributed.

I was inspired to undertake this project by my work on the Children in Urban America Project, an NEH-funded digital archive on the history of children and youth in Milwaukee from the 1850s to the present.

During the four years of gathering, digitizing, and posting documents, I had the pleasure of supervising more than two dozen graduate student researchers, to whom I dedicate this book: Brigitte Charaus, Gretchen Cochrane, John Degnitz, Paula Dicks, Jodi Bartley Eastberg, Paul Ferguson, Jason Feucht, Jason Hostutler, Gayle Kiszely, Steve Lane, Chris Lehman, John McCarthy, Erin McGrath, Christopher Miller, Enaya Othman, Aaron Palmer, Amy Bedford Peters, Melissa Prickett, Candice Quinn, Wayne Riggs, Katie Sanders, Richard Schueler, Shannon Speese, Heather Stur, Julie Tatlock, and Daryl Webb. Special thanks goes to Karen Kehoe, who served as associate director and den mother of the project for two years.

James Marten

Contents

Foreword   v

Preface   vii

PART ONE
Introduction: The Child in the City   1

Toward an Ideal Childhood   5
How the Other Half Lives   10
A Right to Childhood   13
Cultures of Children and Youth   22

PART TWO
The Documents   27

1. The "Dangerous Classes"   29

Changing Attitudes toward Urban Children, 1872–1909   29

1. Charles Loring Brace, *The Dangerous Classes of New York, and Twenty Years' Work among Them,* 1872   30
2. Jacob Riis, *How the Other Half Lives,* 1890   33
3. Jane Addams, *The Spirit of Youth and the City Streets,* 1909   39

Studies of City Boys and Girls   **43**

  4. Vice Commission of the City of Chicago,
     The Social Evil in Chicago: Study of Existing
     Conditions with Recommendations, 1911   43

  5. Chicago Commission on Race Relations,
     The Negro in Chicago: A Study of Race Relations
     and a Race Riot, 1922   49

  6. Emory S. Bogardus, *The City Boy and His Problems:*
     A Survey of Boy Life in Los Angeles, 1926   59

Studies of Children at Work   **63**

  7. E. N. Clopper, *Children on the Streets of Cincinnati,*
     1908   64

  8. United States Children's Bureau, *Industrial Home*
     Work of Children, 1922   71

"We Are Devouring the Boys and Girls":
The Campaign against Child Labor   **76**

  9. Ernest H. Crosby, *The Machines,* 1902   76

 10. Child Labor Bulletin, *The Story of My Cotton Dress,*
     August 1913   79

 11. Lewis Hine and the National Child Labor
     Committee, *Images of Children at Work,* 1908–1921   81

2. A Right to Childhood   **88**

The Nurture and Protection of Children   **88**

 12. Edward T. Devine, *The Right View of the Child,*
     April 25, 1908   89

Case Studies of Progressive Reform   **93**

 13. Lilian V. Robinson, *The City of Hawthorne,*
     November 4, 1905   93

 14. Walter E. Kruesi, *The School of Outdoor Life*
     for Tuberculous Children, December 19, 1909   99

 15. Felix J. Koch, *Little Mothers of Tomorrow,*
     October 1917   102

The School as a Social Settlement 106

16. John Dewey and Evelyn Dewey, *Schools of To-Morrow*, 1915 107

Juvenile Justice 113

17. Benjamin B. Lindsey, *The Dangerous Life*, 1931 114

18. Helen Rankin Jeter, *The Chicago Juvenile Court*, 1922 117

"The Day of the Child Has Come": The Chicago Child Welfare Exhibit, 1911 123

19. Cyrus H. McCormick, *Introductory Remarks*, 1911 124

20. Chicago Child Welfare Exhibit, *Team Work for City Boys*, 1911 126

21. Chicago Child Welfare Exhibit, *Child Health and Welfare*, 1911 129

22. *Images from the Chicago Child Welfare Exhibit*, 1911 136

3. The Spirit of Youth 140

The Newsboys' World 140

23. The Newsboys' World, *Stick!* March 1916 141

24. The Newsboys' World, *Lest We Forget*, January 1921 142

25. The Newsboys' World, *What Is Required of the Ideal Successful Newsboy?* April 1927 143

Delinquent Childhoods 145

26. Vice Commission of the City of Chicago, *Tantine's Story*, 1911 146

27. Clifford R. Shaw, *The Jack-Roller: A Delinquent Boy's Own Story*, 1930 149

Remembered Childhoods 155

28. Golda Meir, *My Life*, 1975 156

29. Josephine Baker, *Josephine*, 1976 161

30. Langston Hughes, *The Big Sea: An Autobiography*, 1940 168

APPENDIXES

A Chronology of Child Welfare Reforms in the Progressive Era (1853–1938)   172

Questions for Consideration   176

Selected Bibliography   178

Index   183

PART ONE

Introduction:
The Child in the City

On a hot day in May 1911, Susan Glaspell, a Chicago journalist and playwright, turned down the chance to go for a drive and went instead to the Chicago Coliseum, where she toured the Child Welfare Exhibit. Organized by the famous social welfare reformer Jane Addams and a host of other Chicago activists and philanthropists, the exhibit aimed to educate the public about the heartbreaking conditions facing many American children and about some of the programs developed by private organizations and government agencies to combat them. Glaspell went "because I thought I ought to go. One should know all that one should about those things, said I to myself." As a result, "with a pleasing sense of my own virtue," she joined tens of thousands of other Chicagoans streaming into the sweltering old building.

Glaspell discovered the exhibit to be a compelling demonstration of the conditions facing city children. "It was a great thing to do—thus to assemble the thing before our very eyes; the full horror of conditions as they are now, what is being done, what might be done, *will* be done, this makes us hope." She strolled past booths, posters, and demonstrations created by hospitals and schools, settlement houses and Boys Clubs, parks administrators and orphanages. At one point she stopped in front of the Chicago Health Department exhibit. She found herself annoyed by a flashing red light, until she realized that each flash represented the death of a child some place in the world from a preventable disease. That moment of realization was not

1

"spoiled" by "preaching." Here, Glaspell wrote, and throughout the exhibit, the posters and displays "told it in a way that gets you. I watched woman after woman stand before it and then turn away with dimmed eyes." The exhibit was designed to inspire just that mixture of grief and interest, to create awareness as well as outrage.[1]

Glaspell was struck by the displays on childhood illness and mortality, and she took particular meaning from "watching the people as they did their seeing. One could fairly see the thoughts forming in their minds as they looked from things as they are to things as some wise brave men and women are struggling to make them." Although the exhibit gave her hope, she assured readers that "it doesn't spare our feelings in showing how bad things are now." Nevertheless, "you come away more inspired than disheartened, for it had shown you that great things are being done for children, and that the end is not yet." She closed with a graceful, optimistic summary of what the exhibit had accomplished: "The Child Welfare exhibit is a meeting ground for adults. It is a breeding place for thoughts. It is Science placing her gifts in the outstretched hands of Democracy."[2]

Glaspell's elegant phrase—"Science placing her gifts in the outstretched hands of Democracy"—captured perfectly the ways that early-twentieth-century reformers hoped they could improve the lives of American children. The Child Welfare Exhibit was held at the height of the Progressive Era, which lasted from the 1890s through the First World War. Many of the ideas put forward during this time had been brewing for years and would continue to influence reformers and policy makers for decades (in fact, several of the documents in this book were written in the 1920s). But the Progressive Era remains a unique historical period, the first of several periods of reform and innovation in the twentieth century.

Progressivism attracted men and women of all political persuasions; both the Democrat Woodrow Wilson and the Republican Theodore Roosevelt considered themselves Progressives. But uniting all Progressives was what Roosevelt called a "fierce discontent of evil"—of those people and forces that worked against fairness, justice, and equality in the United States. To combat this evil, Progressives placed their confidence in scientific research—one must find out what is wrong before one can change it—and in the capacity of professionally trained experts to manage and reform social problems. Another common Progressive belief was that local, state, and federal governments must take the lead in establishing a fair economy, raising the standard of living for everyone, and bringing the nation's vast resources to bear on the many problems facing Americans, especially in the crowded cities.[3]

Progressive reforms at the national level included regulating trusts, lowering tariffs on imports, achieving women's suffrage, prohibiting alcohol, regulating the packaging of food and the sale of drugs, and preserving the environment. At the state level, Progressives established processes for holding referendums to consider legislation, for recalling elected officials, and for regulating child labor. At the local level, reformers in many cities reduced the size of city councils, hired city managers to break the power of corrupt political bosses, and made public utilities out of urban transportation, power, and sewer systems.

There were many causes and inspirations for this coming together of diverse political parties and interest groups. Some reformers were concerned by the soaring number of foreigners flooding American cities, others by the expanding gulf between the rich and poor, still others by the disorder caused by political corruption and labor strife. Although Progressives did not completely ignore rural America, they were far more interested in the chaotic cities bursting with immigrants and social problems. Many acted out of compassion for the less fortunate, while others feared that without a coherent approach to poverty, crime, political corruption, and urban hygiene, to name only a few targets of change, society was in danger of falling apart. The only solution was to impose discipline and fairness on society. Progressives were engaged, in the famous words of the historian Robert H. Wiebe, in a "search for order," and the programs they designed to confront the problems of the cities reflected that imperative.[4] Similar motivations led to conflicting results, however. For instance, whereas northern political reformers aimed to "clean up" politics by eliminating city bosses, southern Progressives sought to "clean up" the violence and corruption in their states by disfranchising the African Americans against whom most of that violence and corruption was directed.

Child welfare became the issue that most Progressives could agree on. The most popular reforms among Progressive activists were related to children: juvenile justice, playgrounds, pensions for widowed mothers, health care, housing. Even child labor laws received almost unanimous support from the various branches of the Progressive movement. As innocent victims and as the hope for America's future, children had to be protected. They represented all that was good about the country, and the way they were treated reflected the nation's values and priorities.[5]

Another characteristic of Progressive thought that deeply affected child welfare efforts was nostalgia for the small towns in which many reformers had grown up. The Boston social worker Philip Davis, in his widely read *Street-Land: Its Little People and Big Problems,* revealed a powerful longing for the values and conditions of small towns in arguing that the "sights and sounds" of the city "are foreign to ideal childhood. Beauty is everywhere suppressed. Birds and flowers are mere spelling words to many city children. Dull and loud colors blur each other. Wild noises fill the air." Americans' affection for traditional small towns—like the little Illinois town in which Jane Addams lived as a girl—would spur Progressives to create programs characterized by interpersonal contact, wholesome entertainment and leisure activities, and a sometimes naïve sense of fair play.[6]

A final element of the Progressive mind-set was the Social Gospel movement that emerged in the United States in the 1880s. Led by Protestant clergy and lay activists and advocated by many Roman Catholic priests and Jewish rabbis, the Social Gospel grew from the recognition that not all Americans benefited equally from the American economic and political systems. The sometimes bloody labor unrest that plagued the country from the 1870s through the 1890s reflected deep divisions in American society; unlike the businessmen who crushed labor unions and the politicians who sent troops to put down strikes, reformers believed that understanding and compassion for the working and immigrant classes would be much more effective than force. Progressives as different as Theodore Roosevelt and Jane Addams were guided at least in part by their religious faith, which inspired them to use public and private resources to bring fairness and hope into the lives of the underprivileged and foreign-born.

These assumptions led reformers to construct fairly narrow paths through which all children were supposed to pass. They often ignored ethnic, religious, and economic differences in their efforts to ensure that all children shared the same opportunities and enjoyed the same advantages. But they did not ignore race. African Americans were encouraged to participate in Progressive reforms, but they did so in segregated facilities and organizations. And despite the fact that most reformers were not working on behalf of a particular religious denomination, moral indignation influenced their perceptions and ideals. The goals of the new generation of reformers might not include conversion, but they certainly included a well-developed sense of right and wrong and a moral imperative that would have been familiar to earlier, denomination-based reformers. Indeed, the facts uncovered by re- formers' surveys, seemingly objective interview techniques, and com- pilation of statistics were often accompanied by sentimental and judgmental language condemning corporations, ignorant and abusive parents (mostly immigrants), and uncaring and corrupt local govern- ments.

TOWARD AN IDEAL CHILDHOOD

Observers had not always been so sympathetic to the poor and needy children in American cities. In 1849, New York City's chief of police, George W. Matsell, reported on the "increasing number of vagrants, idle and vicious children of both sexes, who infest our public thor- oughfares, hotels, docks" and "are growing up in ignorance and profli- gacy." These youngsters, he predicted, were "destined to a life of misery, shame and crime, and ultimately to a felon's doom." The chief blamed their "always careless, generally intemperate and oftentimes immoral and dishonest parents" for the plight of the children, but nev- ertheless complained that the youngsters, who were "addicted to immoralities of the most loathsome description," had become a "fes- tering fountain," creating "a ceaseless stream to our lowest brothels, to the penitentiary and the state's prison."[7]

Two generations later the Swedish sociologist Ellen Key declared that the twentieth century would be the "Century of the Child," an era of understanding and compassion. She promoted educational pro- cesses that depended less on rote learning and more on the ways that children actually learned; encouraged parents, especially mothers, to take a more active interest in their children; and argued that better parenting and schooling would not only lead to better lives for chil- dren, but would also solve long-standing social problems and create a better world. American reformers embraced Key's optimism and ideas and frequently borrowed the phrase, which reflected their high hopes and serious purposes.

The vast differences in the attitudes expressed by Matsell and Key reflect the shift in ideas about children that had been developing for decades before the Progressive Era. Although only a minority of American children could enjoy it, the optimistic, nurturing, and child- centered ideal became a powerful model to which many Americans aspired. More important, the assumptions it contained were applied to the problems facing city children by most urban reformers, at least some of whom believed that there was an "ideal" childhood and that society should enable all children to live that ideal.

The rise of this "child-nurture" philosophy of child rearing was directly linked to the growth of the urban middle class, which dominated the reform movements of the Progressive Era. Then, as now, the term *middle class* was somewhat hard to define. Ranking below the "upper 10 percent," as the wealthy were often called, but above the struggling working classes, the middle class comprised small businesspeople and bureaucrats, independent farmers and urban professionals, white-collar workers and teachers, clerks and small manufacturers. A recent history of Progressivism argues that these diverse groups united in their concern over the deterioration of the social fabric in the United States, which they blamed on the indifference of the upper class and the poverty of the lower class. The middle class characterized the wealthiest Americans as parasites and criticized their excessive, thoughtless consumption of resources and contempt for traditional family values (they divorced regularly and exiled their children to boarding schools). The working poor, however debased their lifestyles, were largely seen to be the victims of ignorance and powerlessness. Both groups needed to be reformed, and although middle-class Progressives did promote reforms directed at the wealthy—making divorce more difficult, for instance—they spent most of their time on repairing the lives of the poor.[8]

Middle-class reformers thought about childhood in the context of their own lives and attitudes. And although they did focus some of their energy on children from their own class—on public schools, especially—they also projected their images of the ideal childhood onto the working class. However, the comfort, safety, and security that the expanding middle class was able to provide for its children and that had come to be associated with a "normal" childhood were almost impossible to achieve for working-class families, especially in American cities. In other words, many Progressive child welfare programs were inspired by living standards that the middle class had come to expect and that working-class and most immigrant families could hardly dream of.

For instance, the number of children born to American families decreased markedly during the century after 1820. In 1830, there were 128 people under the age of twenty for every 100 people twenty and over (among whites). By 1890, the number had plunged to seventy-nine; in 1920 it was only sixty-six. In urban areas, the decline was even more dramatic, to only fifty-six young people for every 100 adults in 1920. But immigrant families and many working-class families continued to have large numbers of children, and the percentage of young people under the age of twenty living in American cities remained as high as 45 percent.[9]

These statistics are important because reformers typically commented on the large number of children in the neediest families. And they could not help but compare the desperation of those families' lives to their own comfortable existence. By the turn of the twentieth century the steady decline in family size had already produced significant changes in child-rearing practices and in the material lives of children. They were given more room—literally and figuratively—and enjoyed greater privacy and opportunities to develop their own interests. Beginning in the mid-nineteenth century, the commercial publishing and toy industries began to take over the play and leisure time of children. Nurseries and children's bedrooms were filled with mass-produced toys and books and magazines published exclusively for children. From lurid dime novels and the titillating fare of nickelodeons to the slightly more respectable and uplifting stories of Horatio Alger and ever-popular magazines like *Youth's Companion,* children, especially in cities and towns, had more entertainment options than ever before. One poll in 1911 discovered that, on any given day in New York City, one out of eight children attended a movie. Even more spectacular were the amusement parks opening around the country at the turn of the century, including Coney Island, which drew a million people— many of them youngsters and teenagers—every summer.

Conversely, although poor children were also eager consumers of movies and other cheap entertainment, they and their families enjoyed few other urban comforts. As middle-class families moved into roomy townhouses or bungalows in the suburbs, the poor in American cities were lucky to get a tiny apartment, where six, eight, or perhaps a dozen family members crowded into two rooms—and sometimes took in boarders. More than 80,000 tenements housed millions of New York City dwellers by 1900. These five- or six-story, poorly constructed buildings were divided into tiny apartments with no indoor plumbing, rows of dilapidated outdoor toilets crowded in back of the building, and severely inadequate ventilation. The Jewish section on the Lower East Side contained half a million people per square mile, one of the highest population densities in history. New York's housing situation was more extreme than that in most cities, but all the fast-growing urban areas in the industrial North were plagued by deteriorating neighborhoods, where largely immigrant populations were crammed into substandard housing.[10]

Another set of opposing factors helps explain both Progressivism and the problems that Progressives sought to eradicate. Combined with a general rise in income, especially among the urban middle class, smaller family size made it easier to stretch material and emotional resources, raising the standard of living for many children and enabling more Americans to nurture their children properly. Fewer children had to work outside the home; more could go to school for longer periods of time; and more could benefit from the social and cultural opportunities that abounded in the city. Rather than measuring the value of children by the work they could do or the income they could produce—traditional measures of the "worth" of children, especially in agricultural societies—the urban middle class drew value from the emotional relationships parents formed with their children. This emotional investment in children was reflected in the increasing importance placed on expensive funerals for deceased children and other symbolic manifestations of affection and devotion. At the community level, it was reflected in the public outrage over the deaths of children in automobile and streetcar accidents during the first two decades of the twentieth century.[11]

Although working-class parents also cherished their children, they simply could not afford to keep them out of the workforce. Between 1870 (the first year in which the U.S. Census recorded child labor) and 1900, the percentage of children between the ages of ten and fourteen who worked for wages increased from 16 percent to 22 percent (it was probably higher), and those figures did not account for the tens of thousands who labored in the "street trades" or as tenement-bound "home workers." Advocates for stricter child labor laws highlighted the injuries and long-term health problems caused by working in coal mines, cotton mills, and foundries, as well as the lack of educational and cultural opportunities available to child workers. Of course, the statistics were more complicated than reformers let on: They did not include the large percentage of child laborers who worked on farms. This was another case of middle-class Americans' belief in the benefits of rural living and outdoor work, which were thought to be inherently more healthy and more likely to build character than urban and factory labor. But the percentage of working children who lived in cities rose dramatically between 1870 and 1920, from 47 percent to nearly 75 percent. An early-twentieth-century study of several cities discovered 17,669 children selling newspapers; the Department of Commerce estimated in 1916 that "junkers"—mostly children—collected $265 million worth of scrap metal and ten million pounds of wastepaper. Untold thousands did home work in the meager apartments they shared with their families, producing clothing, placing snaps and buttons on cards, stringing rosary beads, setting stones in cheap jewelry, packaging shoelaces, and making artificial flowers, often for no more than five cents per hour.[12]

Health was yet another factor in the development of middle-class attitudes about the working class and reform. At a time when antibiotics were unknown, few people were immunized for any diseases other than smallpox, pasteurized milk was not widely available, and refrigeration was unreliable at best. Preventing illness and recovering from injuries were often difficult. But the suffering did not affect all children equally. Infant and child mortality rates were higher in cities than in the country and higher among the poor than among the middle and upper classes. Crowded, drafty, and poorly ventilated apartments guaranteed that flu and other illnesses would ensnare entire families; inadequate sewers and garbage removal created breeding grounds for germ-carrying flies and mosquitoes; a rudimentary understanding of nutrition often led doctors to recommend only limited breast-feeding and mothers to regularly feed infants hard-to-digest meat, pickles, and other adult foods; and still-developing notions about infectious diseases and the "germ theory" led even respected pediatricians to prescribe cathartics like castor oil for diarrhea (just the opposite of the treatment necessary for the dehydration-causing digestive illnesses).

Although the statistics are sketchy—the Census Bureau did not begin collecting data on infant mortality until 1900, and then only in ten northern states and selected cities—infant and child mortality was very high at the turn of the century. More than 12 percent of children died before their first birthday, and another 5.7 percent died before they reached the age of five. (By comparison, the infant mortality rate in the United States for 2001 was less than 1 percent.) The most common causes of death, in order, were debility and injuries in newborns (at a time when postnatal care was extremely limited, premature births were a major problem), digestive illnesses, and respiratory problems. For children under the age of five, pneumonia and other respiratory ailments were responsible for a third of all deaths, and measles, scarlet fever, and diphtheria also killed many young children. These diseases—which are prevented by immunizations or cured with powerful drugs today—were virtually untreatable early in the twentieth century. Although all levels of society suffered from these childhood maladies, especially epidemics of diphtheria and flu that could flash through whole communities in a matter of days, the urban poor suffered the most. Studies completed in the early 1910s found that the infant mortality rate was 22 percent in families where the father's annual wages were less than $50 per family member, whereas it was "only" 6 percent in families where the breadwinner earned at least $400 per family member.[13]

Middle-class reformers were horrified by these statistics, and they took note of the obvious differences between the conditions in which they lived and the conditions in which less fortunate Americans lived. Indeed, it is impossible to overestimate the influence of class on the Progressive reformers. They believed middle-class models of childhood and child rearing could—and should—be secured for all children, and tended to ignore cultural, economic, and religious differences in reaching their goals.

Affluent, compassionate Americans often referred to their poorer counterparts as "the other half." The phrase was made famous in Jacob Riis's 1890 book, *How the Other Half Lives,* a scathing description of the sad and debased lives of New York City's neediest residents. (The title comes from an old English saying that "one half of the world does not know how the other half lives.") The phrase also appeared in the headline of a Chicago *Tribune* article about the Child Welfare Exhibit: "Crystallizing Theories into Simple Facts at the Welfare Exhibit, That the First Half May Know How the Other Half Lives." The reporter described the middle- and upper-class women— with their "soft voice[s]" and "gay silk dress[es]" arguing about milk and nutrition with the dozens of poor mothers—"shabby, bareheaded except for an occasional shawl over their heads"—who clustered around the booth. At first, wrote the reporter, the poor women resisted the notion that beer and cabbage were not appropriate foods for babies. But they changed their minds after seeing waxen models of sickly and healthy children, after reading information about the benefits of drinking milk, and after hearing "sharp" words from the well-to-do demonstrator. The article stated confidently that none of the women who visited that booth "will ever feed beer to a baby again."[14]

HOW THE OTHER HALF LIVES

Although "the other half" was, of course, simply a metaphor, Progressives were serious about studying the lives of poor Americans and creating programs to assist them. In fact, a hallmark of the Progressive approach was a compulsion to do research, to identify and articulate problems before developing solutions. Perhaps nothing reflected the middle-class assumptions of child welfare reformers—and their attitudes about the proper relationships between parents and children and the best ways for children to spend their leisure time—than the numerous studies they conducted on child labor. The most popular subjects of their research were newsboys. Reformers conducted at least sixteen studies of newsboys (sometimes including other street traders), in cities such as New York, Cincinnati, Dallas, and Milwaukee, between 1910 and 1925. Although thousands of children worked in southern mills (in small towns or rural areas), in northern sweatshops, and in tenement apartments, doing "home work" with their parents, one of the most prominent faces of child labor for urban Americans was the ubiquitous newsboy. From the 1850s through the 1920s newsboys were responsible for selling millions of newspapers each day. Their romantic, carefree lives were celebrated in dime novels and movies. Even reformers admitted that it was sometimes hard to get the public to understand that newsboys and other street traders were not simply spunky entrepreneurs, but child laborers with little control over their work. Although a majority of newsboys actually lived with their parents, they nevertheless became the symbol of city children who were denied the kind of childhoods that middle-class reformers believed every child had the "right" to enjoy. They also showed how easy it was for boys to slip into a world of dissolution and crime, which could lead to serious problems for the entire society. "If we do not lift him up," wrote one anxious organizer of newsboys, "he will pull us down."[15]

The concern with the moral development of children emerged in another set of studies on how boys and girls spent their leisure time. In reports based on interviews with juvenile delinquents, surveys of school children, and the comments of teachers, social workers, and parents, researchers in cities as small as Springfield, Illinois, and as large as Cleveland, Ohio, and Los Angeles, found that the lack of recreational options led children to inappropriate behavior and even to crime. Studies presented vignettes of boys and girls idling away their time and, in many cases, descending into juvenile delinquency. A Cleveland boy interviewed at the State Industrial School claimed that he spent at least eleven hours a day "in the streets, at the movies, in the railroad yards, and at the 'athletic club'"—actually a pool hall. He also liked going to burlesque shows for the "good jokes" and dancing, and to a local amusement park. Without a neighborhood playground or baseball team, he turned to petty thievery, breaking into freight cars and stealing fruit and, in one escapade, ten cases of ginger ale. His first trip to the State Industrial School was for chronic truancy, being "a general nuisance in the neighborhood"; the second was for breaking into cars. That this boy was out of control seemed confirmed by his statement, "My people never knew, when I left home in the morning, whether I was going to school or not." All of this had happened before he turned fifteen. The inadequacy of recreational facilities—and of children's awareness of even the meager facilities that were available—was highlighted in the story of an eleven-year-old girl who "never drew books from the library, never used playgrounds, and did not know what a park looked like." She was in court because of her relationship with men who worked at the railroad freight yard. The men gave the girl and her friends toys, candy, money, and coal (for their families) in return for unnamed sexual favors. When the girl was asked how often she went to the woods, she replied, "I don't know what a woods is."[16]

Progressives also established a number of associations that published journals on the specific needs of children and youth. Reflecting the movement's commitment to the professionalization of child welfare, these organizations and the journals they published included the New York Charity Organization Society (COS), whose *Charities and the Commons* covered a wide variety of reforms and activities from all over the country; the Federated Boys' Clubs, which published *Work with Boys,* a report of the activities and projects carried out by Boys Clubs around the country; the Playground Association of America, which produced *The Playground*; the National Congress of Mothers (later the Parent Teacher Association), which published *Child Welfare* magazine; and the National Child Labor Committee, which published the *Child Labor Bulletin.*

Reformers regularly held conferences—the most prominent was the annual National Conference on Charities and Corrections—on health and legal issues, playground development, nutrition, and education. Settlement houses like Hull House sponsored workshops for welfare workers and parents alike, and the General Federation of Women's Clubs and the National Congress of Mothers advocated for more federal support of children's issues. In 1911 New York City and Chicago hosted well-attended child welfare exhibits on the problems facing children and ways to solve them. A symbol of the federal government's increasing involvement in children's issues was the White House Conference on Dependent Children, called by President

Theodore Roosevelt and held in Washington early in 1909. Attended by more than two hundred child welfare experts, the two-day meeting examined the problems facing children, discussed possible solutions, and declared that the twentieth century would be the century of the child.

The men and women who founded these organizations, attended their conferences, and wrote for their publications were professional journalists, social workers, and experts in a number of fields related to urban life. A modern American might call them "policy wonks" who had broken free from the amateur, religious-oriented reformism of the nineteenth century. They were less judgmental than their counterparts in previous generations, more interested in the well-being than the souls of the people they were trying to help, and dedicated to bringing private and public resources at the local, state, and federal levels to bear on social problems.

A RIGHT TO CHILDHOOD

Florence Kelley, one of the leading advocates for children at the turn of the century, coined a phrase in 1905 that became another motto for advocates for children and youth during this period and beyond when she asserted that Americans must mobilize to protect "a right to childhood."[17] Of course, there had always been informal, private, limited efforts to help children. Cities often held "poor children's days," treating newsboys, residents of orphanages, and other underprivileged children to a parade, free food, and entertainment. In 1893, hundreds of children paraded through downtown Chicago, crowded onto a train that took them to a field on the South Side, feasted and played games, and finished the day by attending a special performance of Buffalo Bill's "Wild West Show."[18] The reform-minded magazine *The Delineator* took on the plight of orphaned and abandoned children in 1907 with its Child-Rescue Campaign, in which the magazine published adorable pictures and glowing descriptions of small children currently living in institutions who were available for adoption. Prior to the Gilded Age and the Progressive Era, child welfare issues were addressed by private institutions or individuals rather than local, state, or federal governments. These private efforts continued in the twentieth century. There were 1,151 institutions for dependent children in the United States in 1910; most were supported by private societies or religious denominations, which often "placed out" the children to shops, factories, or farms. The late nineteenth and early twentieth centuries also saw the heyday of the famous "orphan trains," sponsored by Charles Loring Brace's New York–based Children's Aid Society. Between the 1850s and 1920s these trains carried as many as 150,000 urban children to live with western families. As private efforts on behalf of the least fortunate city dwellers grew, public contributions dwindled. During the twenty years before 1900, city governments slashed or eliminated entirely their budgets for "outdoor relief"—the only direct aid to poor residents living outside poorhouses, county farms, and other institutions for the temporary housing of the poor.

Despite this retrenchment by city governments, some states became increasingly involved in the care of poor children, foreshadowing the more active government programs that developed after 1930. After the Civil War, for instance, most northern state governments housed orphans and so-called "half orphans" (children who had lost a mother or a father) of Union veterans at soldiers' orphans' homes. Although most of these homes closed in the 1870s and 1880s, a few—notably in Illinois and Indiana—branched out to become the primary state-funded institutions for dependent children. The federal government also made tentative efforts to help the children of Union veterans with a system of widows' and orphans' pensions.

Although Progressives targeted most aspects of children's lives, the campaigns that were most relevant to urban youth addressed children's health, juvenile justice, and child labor issues. Nineteenth-century reformers had initiated a number of efforts on behalf of urban children, from the Children's Aid Societies that sought homes for orphaned or needy children to the Societies for the Prevention of Cruelty to Children that were first organized in American cities in the 1870s.

Also confronting the effect of urban poverty on children were the settlement houses that began appearing in American cities in the late 1880s. In 1889 Jane Addams founded one of the first settlement houses in the United States in an old mansion on Chicago's West Side. She and her partner, Ellen Gates Starr, named their settlement Hull House, and although it was not primarily aimed at children, because of the large concentration of young people in the immigrant neighborhoods surrounding Hull House, it became a center of child welfare efforts in Chicago. Indeed, Addams used Hull House as a base of operations for her leadership in a number of reform efforts, from regulation of child labor to the passage of compulsory education laws. Hull House was a pioneer in other quieter, smaller child welfare efforts. For instance, it organized a kindergarten in the 1890s and, in 1893, Chicago's first public playground. Over the years, its clubs, rural camps, child care programs, and other services for the young became extremely popular. The settlement house movement expanded rapidly, until by 1910 there were more than 400 settlements around the country.[19]

The settlement houses were, in many ways, the precursors of most Progressive Era child welfare reforms. Indeed, many settlement house programs were related to the health of children, one of the most important priorities for urban Progressives. Progressives initiated a number of medical and educational programs revolving around prenatal, infant, and child care. Departments of health in a number of cities sent visiting nurses into slum neighborhoods, set up aid stations (sometimes called "baby tents") to provide clean, well-ventilated, temporary child care, and instructed young girls in nutrition, personal hygiene, and rudimentary child development as part of the so-called Little Mothers' Movement.

The culmination of the campaign to utilize the resources of the federal government to address children's health issues was the creation of the United States Children's Bureau within the Department of Commerce and Labor in 1912. Julia C. Lathrop was named first head of the agency, and although she had a tiny budget (only $25,000 in the first year) and a small staff, over the next thirty years the bureau—the first federal agency in the world dedicated to children—conducted research on child labor and health issues, published pamphlets on child rearing and nutrition, and sponsored events celebrating infant and children's health. One of the bureau's successes was convincing Congress to pass the Sheppard-Towner Act in 1921, which appropriated $7 million to establish local departments of maternity and infant hygiene. During its first three decades of existence, the bureau published scores of studies on child care, child heath, and child labor. Some historians of the bureau, however, are critical of its focus on a narrowly middle-class set of values and assumptions and on its framing of child welfare as a "woman's issue." These approaches, as well as the failure of the federal government to support its programs with adequate resources, hindered the effectiveness of the bureau and made its eventual absorption into other federal agencies inevitable.[20]

Despite its limited accomplishments, the bureau was an important source of information about children's health. Reformers had long believed that one of the greatest causes of poor health among infants and children was ignorance, especially among poor, immigrant groups whose child-rearing practices were patterned after traditional approaches that had long been discredited by science. The bureau initiated baby week campaigns, providing flyers, publicity, how-to bulletins, posters, and other items to state and local organizations. Organizations including public health departments, the Camp Fire Girls, agricultural college extension services, women's groups, hospitals, county governments, churches, and chambers of commerce sponsored baby week events. Generally held in the spring, the events varied dramatically from community to community, but generally included exhibits, lectures, stereopticon displays, and demonstrations on nutrition, the importance of pasteurized milk, creating healthy environments (with adequate ventilation and screened windows, for instance), vaccinations, clothing, and traffic safety. Many baby weeks included competitions for the best slogans, most creative posters and poetry, and essays on child health. Some held "better mothers" contests whose winners earned the best score on child care examinations. Some gave awards to the healthiest babies, who were presented at festive pageants and featured in laudatory newspaper articles. Indeed, the baby contests became one of the most popular—and, because of their exploitative nature, controversial—parts of the campaign.[21]

Progressive efforts to improve public health clearly had humanitarian motives. Juvenile delinquency, the second major concern of child welfare reformers in turn-of-the-century cities, inspired not only compassion for youths, but also fear for the safety of the larger society. Emerging ideas about delinquency and juvenile justice were part of a larger movement to force society as a whole to take responsibility for crime and to allow the expanding court system, particularly low-level municipal courts, to "manage" minor crimes and civil cases. The rising interest in the plight of delinquents led to a wide-ranging battery of reforms, from juvenile courts to organized playgrounds to Boys Clubs. Although the concern about delinquency centered on a criminal justice system that treated young defendants and convicts the same way it treated adults, reformers actually created a coherent program designed to prevent delinquency as well as to rehabilitate juveniles after they ran afoul of the law. Many of these programs reflected the middle-class assumptions that shaped other campaigns. The programs also generally ignored girls, regarding delinquency as the "boy problem." One particular reform that did affect girls was related to a concern over the moral development of juvenile boys: Between the 1880s and 1920 every state of the union raised the age of consent for sexual intercourse from between ten or twelve years to sixteen or eighteen years of age.[22]

The link between delinquency and spare time—made explicit in the studies of how children and youth spent their leisure time—was an important subtext in the playground movement that began in the 1880s and 1890s. The playground movement was responsible for the creation of local associations that hired supervisors for school playgrounds during the summer months, published guides to group games and activities, formed baseball teams, created ice skating rinks and sand piles, and lobbied schools and cities to include recreational facilities in their budgets. Numerous organizations participated in the playground movement, including settlement houses, the Woman's Christian Temperance Union, and women's clubs; in Philadelphia the Culture Extension League, the Civic Club, and the City Park Association all took part. An Outdoor Recreation League was formed in New York City, where in 1898 the school board opened two dozen school playgrounds during the summer under the supervision of 153 directors and assistants. By 1908, reported *Charities and the Commons,* 185 cities maintained supervised playgrounds, two-thirds of them funded by local governments. The professionalization of recreation and play was an important part of the playground movement. In addition to publishing a journal, the Playground Association of America held periodic "play congresses," where delegates discussed and held workshops on funding, the training of supervisors, the design of parks and play apparatus, the organization of day camps and excursions for children, the effect of organized play and playgrounds on juvenile delinquency, and efforts to pass laws regulating playgrounds and recreational facilities.[23]

Both boys and girls benefited from the playground movement, but boys remained the chief target for reformers concerned with the lack of good recreational options. "The boy problem is one of the most important and most difficult problems of the present," wrote one observer. "Crowded cities and specialized industrial work have deprived the boy of opportunities for healthful play and wholesome occupation. The street and the alley have become his playground and his lounging place; the pool-room, the cigar-store and the saloon are open to receive him. Our cities have developed without reference to existence or the needs of the boy—the man of the next generation." This attitude inspired a massive effort to solve the "boy problem," which was actually a number of problems: delinquency, lack of affordable recreational facilities, crowded homes, neglectful parents, and the boundless energy of youth.[24]

Boys Clubs became one of the most popular efforts to shape city boys. Several women organized the first club in Hartford, Connecticut, in 1860, but the idea didn't actually take hold until the 1890s. In 1906, the Federated Boys Clubs was formed in Boston with 53 member organizations. Although the clubs frequently offered courses in handicrafts, art, and even English, their primary purpose was to provide safe, wholesome, and supervised recreation. Clubs sponsored baseball teams, held summer camps, provided gymnasiums, and organized outings. In addition, the boys were encouraged to develop a community spirit reflected in the names they chose for themselves: "The Lily Club," "The Yellow Kids," "The Cuban Avengers," "Success Club," "Young Americans," "Loyalty Club," "The Pilgrims," "North Side Boys' Club," and "Clean Street Aids."

Many of the new institutions created for children and youth introduced a limited form of self-government. The most famous was William R. George's "Junior Republic," established in the mid-1890s near Freeville, New York. Guided by the motto "Nothing without labor," the boys (and, later, girls) brought to Freeville by distressed parents or sent there by juvenile court judges lived and worked with adult supervision and discipline. But they also elected dozens of their own representatives, earned money to spend at the republic shop (the republic even produced its own currency for a number of years), and agreed to follow rules established by their elected representatives and judges, to the extent that they could be fined or even sentenced to "jail" for infractions. The Junior Republic normally housed teenagers, but much younger boys, eight to thirteen years old, resided at the "Commonwealth of Ford"—also known as the Ford Republic—outside Detroit. The boys elected to official positions received salaries and status in the community. A thirteen-year-old Ford Republic "judge" became a local celebrity in Detroit, and when he died tragically from a heart ailment the state supreme court sent one of its members to the funeral. The commitment to boys' self-government in the institution became a model for dozens of similar organizations, including the United States of Tacoma in Washington State; the "State of Columbia," established by a boys club in San Francisco; the Boys' Brotherhood Republic in Chicago, which established its own savings bank and employment agency; and "newsboys' republics," created in Milwaukee, Toledo, and other cities, which elected officers, helped regulate newsboys' work, sponsored sports teams and other activities, and, in Milwaukee, published a newspaper.[25]

Organizations like the Boy Scouts, the Girl Scouts, and the Camp Fire Girls also promoted middle-class ideas and provided wholesome entertainment, taught useful skills, and ensured appropriate supervision by adults. The "guardian" of the Cleveland Park Camp Fire in Washington, D.C., reported a wide array of educational and recreational activities for the second half of 1912. In addition to swimming, tennis, roller skating, "outdoor sleeping," and singing, the girls received first-aid and embroidery lessons; heard lectures on hygiene, book illumination, and birds; and visited a book bindery, the U.S. Bureau of Standards, a bakery, and the city's filtration plant and pumping station. These outings were not simply for fun; hour-long examinations followed lectures on subjects like "The Proper Disposal of Waste and Garbage."[26]

The first Boy Scout handbook described the "virtues" that members should learn and reflect: the "Twelve Points of the Scout Law." A Boy Scout must be trustworthy, loyal, helpful, friendly, courteous, kind, obedient, cheerful, thrifty, brave, clean, and reverent. None of these qualities appeared in contemporary descriptions of newsboys, street urchins, "dependent" children, or desperately poor immigrant youth. In a way, the scouting movement was designed to shape children to be just the opposite of what many activists believed to be the typical city child. Indeed, the leading historian of the Boy Scouts and other "character-building agencies" argues that, although inspired by the public image of urban children as delinquents in training, local and national Boy Scout leaders—drawn from the middle class—worked harder to recruit boys from their own class than to recruit poor, immigrant children from the cities. Despite the fairly narrow goals and attitudes animating character building—or, perhaps, because of them—these groups were wildly popular. There were well over 400,000 Boy Scouts by the early 1920s.[27]

Some new organizations sought simply to bring at-risk city children into contact with responsible, adult role models. The Big Brothers and Big Sisters both emerged in the early 1900s, and a short-lived "Caddy Camp" brought a few dozen city boys to a golf resort in the White Mountains of New Hampshire, where they camped out and caddied for wealthy, active men. The idea behind the caddy camp was that the boys would absorb the men's work ethic and other useful values. Similarly, the Wisconsin Home and Farm School aimed to prevent delinquency by taking troubled boys out of the city—mostly from nearby Milwaukee—and teaching them to become good citizens through hard work, close supervision, and tough but loving care. Scores of groups with similar goals emerged around the nation during this period.[28]

Of course, not all city boys and girls had access to such organizations, and some simply refused to take part. Late-nineteenth- and early-twentieth-century Americans believed that something had to be done about juvenile delinquency, especially among boys. One of the most enduring examples of Progressive efforts to balance responsibility with compassion, to distinguish between youth and adults, and to put the government to work on behalf of young people was the establishment of separate court systems for juveniles. Throughout the 1880s and 1890s there had been efforts to ease the treatment of young criminals: The state of Massachusetts held separate hearings for children, some young offenders were put on probation rather than sent to jail, and in a few cities philanthropic organizations organized jailhouse schools for incarcerated youths.

Although the best-known advocate of juvenile courts early in the century was the Denver judge Benjamin Lindsey, women's club members, settlement house workers, and social scientists—united by gender, middle-class assumptions, and a desire to soften juvenile justice with a strong dose of maternalism—led the nineteenth- and early-twentieth-century drive to establish juvenile courts. Female advocates were more willing than their male counterparts to stress the importance of protecting innocent children over protecting society from delinquents. They were also more likely than men to insist on establishing new laws and courts rather than simply work within the existing criminal justice system. Most states adopted their approach; the first court devoted solely to juveniles was created in Chicago in 1899, and by 1920 virtually every state in the union had passed laws establishing special courts, probation systems, and detention homes for juvenile offenders.[29]

The goal of these courts, according to Lindsey, was to defend "the sacred period of adolescence." Reformers believed that treating youthful criminals as adults ignored the social, economic, and cultural causes of their behavior. Moreover, sending them to jail only brought them into contact with hardened adult offenders and inevitably corrupted youths even further. Juvenile court judges, like Lindsey, treated delinquents on a case-by-case basis, weighing the conditions in which they had been raised against the crimes they were accused of committing. Jail sentences were rare; rather, judges tried to counsel the youth who came before them, put them on probation in the custody of a responsible adult, or, if institutionalization was necessary, send them to a reform school rather than jail. An important distinction made by these reform-minded jurists was the difference between a delinquent and a criminal. The former, they believed, could be rehabilitated if treated correctly.[30]

Although juvenile courts were publicized as great child-saver success stories, the facts were more complicated. Critics of the system have accused juvenile courts of being more interested in controlling city youth than in bringing them to justice. In many cases, the "delinquents" brought before the courts had been arrested for activities that were not crimes. A 1913 study of an immigrant neighborhood in New York City revealed that more than half of juvenile arrests were for "begging, bonfires, gambling, jumping on [street]cars, . . . playing with water pistols, putting out lights, selling papers, shooting craps, snowballing, subway disturbances, and throwing stones." Boys and girls alike were brought before juvenile courts on vague charges like "incorrigibility," "immorality," and disorderly conduct. Some parents and teachers simply used the new courts as a way to get troublesome teenagers out of their classrooms and off the street, at least temporarily.

Another major priority for Progressives was the campaign against child labor, which became one of the movement's largest efforts. Throughout the nineteenth century, trade unions had advocated restrictions on child labor, arguing that work deprived children of equal access to education and that the low wages paid to children depressed the wages of working adults. Late in the century the National Consumers League took the lead in the fight against child labor, but many other humanitarian and philanthropic organizations — church groups, women's clubs, settlement houses, and social service organizations — joined the fight. By the turn of the century, child labor committees had been formed in New York, Alabama, and several other states, and by 1903 a number of states had passed significant child labor legislation.

When leaders of these committees and organizations decided to agitate for a national approach to child labor, they formed the National Child Labor Committee (NCLC) in 1904. The NCLC worked to mobilize the public, labor unions, and politicians against child labor. Although it did not focus, strictly speaking, on city children, the NCLC drew much of its support from urban child welfare workers. Its publications highlighted the damage that full-time work could do to children, including lost limbs, respiratory diseases, bent backs, and undeveloped minds. Through investigations and publicity garnered by the work of pioneering photographers like Lewis Hine, the NCLC promoted the enforcement of existing child labor laws and the passage of stricter regulations. The model law promoted by the NCLC was fairly weak by twenty-first-century standards: a minimum age of fourteen for working in factories, and sixteen in mines; an eight-hour day for fourteen- and fifteen-year-old industrial workers; and no night work for youths under the age of sixteen. The resulting Keating-Owen Act of 1916 carried great symbolic value—it incorporated most NCLC goals—but applied to only a fraction of the children employed in the United States. Many southerners opposed the law because it gave the federal government power over the states. Others fought against it because they believed children were better off working in factories than idling on the streets, and that until there were enough schools for youth to attend—southern states lagged far behind northern states in providing postelementary education for their children—they should continue working. The U.S. Supreme Court ruled the Keating-Owen Act unconstitutional only nine months after its passage. Effective federal regulation of child labor would not be implemented until the Fair Labor Standards Act of 1938.[31]

CULTURES OF CHILDREN AND YOUTH

The story of the child in the city would not be complete without the children's own perceptions of city life. As in so many other facets of children's lives, class differences led to the creation of a number of separate cultures of children and youth. One form of youth culture centered in the burgeoning high schools. The first American high school, Boston English, was established in 1821. The number of high schools in the United States grew slowly throughout the nineteenth century, and although the percentage of teenagers in high school remained relatively small, the number of high schoolers increased dramatically during the late nineteenth and early twentieth centuries, from 72,000 in 1870 to more than two million in 1920. Perhaps a third of all fourteen- to seventeen-year-olds attended high school in 1920, and approximately 16 percent actually graduated. Middle- and upper-class boys and girls (in fact, girls constituted a substantial majority of most graduating classes during this time) were far more likely to attend high school than working-class, immigrant, and African American students, although high schools nevertheless became the center of a developing youth culture.[32]

Students established sports teams and debating societies, published school newspapers and yearbooks, ran student governments, and organized dances and other social events. Over time school administrators took control over most student activities in American high schools, establishing conferences for sports teams, requiring coaches, conductors, and other advisers of student activities to be faculty members, limiting participation in official activities (especially sports) to students in good academic standing, and censoring student publications. They created regulated, safe, and structured places that could not have been more different from the wild and woolly environment of the streets.[33]

Only a small minority of teenagers actually attended school, however, and another form of youth culture also flourished on city streets, which became playgrounds for stickball, marbles, hide-and-seek, and various improvised street games. The crowded working-class and immigrant neighborhoods became communities of children, where older siblings watched out for and trained younger children; where games with elaborate rules evolved; where "turf" wars between children of various ethnic groups were common; where dead horses, fires, fights, and accidents provided street drama; where discarded objects became improvised toys—bicycle wheels turned into hoops, bags full of rags into footballs, garbage-pail lids into sleds. Girls claimed the stoops in front of tenements as their territory, where they played house (often while taking care of younger brothers and sisters), and boys owned the streets, where they competed for space with carriages, street merchants' carts, streetcars, and pedestrians. And every block or two they could find a place where, for a few cents, they could watch a scratchy, soundless movie.

Two archetypal city boys represent these two vastly different youth cultures. Claude G. Bowers, who as an adult would be a well-known newspaper editor and columnist, historian, Democratic party leader, and ambassador to Spain and Chile, attended Shortridge High School in Indianapolis in the 1890s. Claude kept a detailed diary with nearly daily reports of his club and class activities. He and his friends were constantly on the go, attending lectures at local colleges and at the high school (speakers included Jane Addams and Booker T. Washington), playing poker, attending the opera and theater, and sightseeing in nearby villages. But Claude and his friends had time for school events, too, and his diary frequently mentions politicking for class offices, formal school debates, the publication of a school literary magazine and yearbook, mock trials, reading clubs, the formation of an oratorical association (he was elected president), the school's annual "Puritan supper" (a kind of Thanksgiving celebration), and other intellectual and social pursuits. He also managed to find time for girls, reporting late in his senior year that he and a friend "once more had engagements with the girls of the Spooners Club, and had a great time as usual, 50 kisses, 3 girls on lap, 25 embraces. Ye Gods! and still we live."[34]

In New York, at about the same time, a little Jewish boy entered the youth culture of the streets. Adolph "Harpo" Marx, who would become the white-wigged, horn-honking but otherwise silent member of the Marx Brothers comedy team, was one of those turn-of-the-century street kids about whom reformers worried so much. Harpo and his brothers Chico and Groucho virtually lived on the streets of New York. School was not a priority of the Marx brothers, who spent their time scrounging for money, gambling, and battling the Irish, German, and Italian boys whose neighborhoods bordered their own Upper East Side Jewish enclave.

"It was all part of the endless fight for recognition of foreigners in the process of becoming Americans," Harpo recalled many years later. "Every Irish kid who made a Jewish kid knuckle under was made to say 'Uncle' by an Italian, who got his lumps from a German kid, who got his insides kicked out by his old man for street fighting and then went out and beat up an Irish kid to heal his wounds." When the boys were not fighting each other, they were cutting a wide swath through the neighborhoods. "Individually and in gangs," Harpo recalled, "we accounted for most of the petty thievery and destruction of property on the Upper East Side," and, as a result, they were "hounded," "harassed," and "chased" by police officers, who "every chance they got, happily beat the hell out of us."

Harpo spent a lot of time in Central Park, searching for lost tennis balls, "sledding" in wintertime on stolen dishpans, and ice skating on a single hand-me-down skate. He also described swimming amid the floating garbage in the East River, making "snazzy" rings out of hairs yanked from brewery horses' tails, "swindling" ticket takers on the "el" in order to get to the Polo Grounds, where he could watch baseball games for free from a bluff overlooking left field (which was, unfortunately, the only part of the field he could see). The family splurged one day each year on an excursion to North Beach in the Bronx. Family members swam, sunbathed, ate watermelon, played in the sand, told jokes, and generally forgot their cares until catching the last ferry home. "It was always a melancholy homecoming," because everyone knew that it would be another year before they could once again leave behind the "hard work and misery" that characterized every other day of the year.[35]

Both Claude and Harpo grew up to lead successful adult lives. But their vastly different backgrounds not only represent the wide range of childhood experiences of Americans in the late nineteenth and early twentieth century—and only the experiences of white males from northern cities—but also suggest some of the differences in perceptions and assumptions of middle-class and working-class Americans. Claude was sophisticated, calm, urbane, a follower of rules who embraced typical ambitions and values. Harpo was a shrewd hustler bent on testing boundaries. Youths like Harpo made adult versions of Claude nervous, but also inspired them to undertake humane, if flawed, efforts to improve the lives of disadvantaged urban children and youth. That tension lies at the center of *Childhood and Child Welfare in the Progressive Era.*

NOTES

[1] Susan Glaspell, "Hearing the Cry of the Children: A Glimpse at the Child Welfare Exhibit," *Morrison's Chicago Weekly,* 3 (May 18, 1911): 14.

[2] Ibid., 14–15.

[3] Quoted in Michael McGerr, *A Fierce Discontent: The Rise and Fall of the Progressive Movement in America, 1870–1920* (New York: Free Press, 2003), vii.

[4] Robert H. Wiebe, *The Search for Order, 1877–1920* (New York: Hill and Wang, 1967).

[5] Ibid., 168–69.

[6] Philip Davis, *Street-Land: Its Little People and Big Problems* (Boston: Small, Maynard & Company, 1915), 47–48.

[7] *Semi-Annual Report of the Chief of Police from May 1 to October 31, 1849* (New York, 1850), 58–61, 62–66.

[8] McGerr, *A Fierce Discontent,* especially 3–39. A recent anthology on the origins and evolution of the American middle class is Burton S. Bledstein and Robert D. Johnston, eds., *The Middling Sorts: Explorations in the History of the American Middle Class* (London: Routledge, 2000).

[9] David I. Macleod, *The Age of the Child: Children in America, 1890–1920* (New York: Twayne, 1998), 3, 5.

[10] Raymond A. Mohl, *The New City: Urban America in the Industrial Age, 1860–1920* (Arlington Heights, Ill.: Harlan Davidson, 1985), 51.

[11] Viviana A. Zelizer, *Pricing the Priceless Child: The Changing Social Value of Children* (New York: Basic Books, 1985).

[12] Hugh D. Hindman, *Child Labor: An American History* (Armonk, N.Y.: M. E. Sharpe, 2002), 31. United States Children's Bureau, *Industrial Home Work of Children* (Washington, D.C.: U.S. Government Printing Office, 1922).

[13] Macleod, *Age of the Child,* 34–41.

[14] Chicago *Tribune,* May 14, 1911.

[15] Quoted in LeRoy Ashby, *Saving the Waifs: Reformers and Dependent Children* (Philadelphia: Temple University Press, 1984), 105.

[16] Henry W. Thurston, *Delinquency and Spare Time: A Study of a Few Stories Written into the Court Records of the City of Cleveland* (New York: William F. Fell, 1918), 28–31, 38–39.

[17]Florence Kelley, *Some Ethical Gains through Legislation* (New York: Macmillan, 1905), 99.

[18]Chicago *Tribune,* July 28, 1893.

[19]The classic study of the settlement house movement is Allen F. Davis, *Spearheads for Reform: The Social Settlements and the Progressive Movement* (New York: Oxford University Press, 1967).

[20]Kriste Lindenmeyer, *"A Right to Childhood": The U.S. Children's Bureau and Child Welfare, 1912–1946* (Urbana: University of Illinois Press, 1997).

[21]U.S. Children's Bureau, *Baby-Week Campaigns, Bureau Publication No. 15* (Washington, D.C.: U.S. Government Printing Office, 1917).

[22]For age-of-consent campaigns, see Mary E. Odem, *Delinquent Daughters: Protecting and Policing Adolescent Female Sexuality in the United States, 1885–1920* (Chapel Hill: University of North Carolina Press, 1995).

[23]"The Playgrounds of 185 cities," *Charities and the Commons,* 21 (Oct. 3, 1908): 4–5. David Macleod cautions that, despite the publicity and activity, most children did not patronize supervised playgrounds; fewer than 4 percent of Cleveland and Milwaukee children and probably fewer than 20 percent of Chicago children utilized playgrounds. Macleod, *Age of the Child,* 66.

[24]Frank T. Carlton, "The Toledo Newsboys' Association," *The Commons* (Sept. 1905): 493.

[25]Ashby, *Saving the Waifs,* 21–22, 133–69.

[26]Helen Buckler and Mary F. Fiedler, *Wo-He-Lo: The Story of Camp Fire Girls, 1910–1960* (New York: Holt, Rinehart and Winston, 1961), 255–56.

[27]Boy Scouts of America, *The Official Handbook for Boys* (Garden City, N.Y.: Doubleday, Page & Co., 1911), 8; David I. Macleod, *Building Character in the American Boy: The Boy Scouts, YMCA, and Their Forerunners, 1870–1920* (Madison: University of Wisconsin Press, 1983).

[28]Ashby, *Saving the Waifs,* 15, 18.

[29]Elizabeth J. Clapp, *Mothers of All Children: Women Reformers and the Rise of Juvenile Courts in Progressive Era America* (University Park: Pennsylvania State University Press, 1998).

[30]Quoted in Macleod, *Age of the Child,* 141.

[31]Hindman, *Child Labor: An American History,* 44–89. The standard account of the NCLC is William I. Trattner, *Crusade for the Children: A History of the National Child Labor Committee and Child Labor Reform in America* (Chicago: Quadrangle Books, 1970).

[32]Macleod, *Age of the Child,* 149.

[33]Reed Ueda, *Avenues to Adulthood: The Origins of the High School and Social Mobility in an American Suburb* (New York: Cambridge University Press, 1987), 120; Macleod, *Age of the Child,* 150–51.

[34]Holman Hamilton and Gayle Thornbrough, *Indianapolis in the "Gay Nineties": High School Diaries of Claude G. Bowers* (Indianapolis: Indiana Historical Society, 1964), quote on 110.

[35]Harpo Marx and Rowland Barber, *Harpo Speaks!* (New York: Bernard Geis, 1961; Limelight Editions, 1985), 36, 46.

PART TWO

The Documents

1

The "Dangerous Classes"

Progressives attacked a wide range of abuses in the American political and economic systems, raised public awareness of social ills, and articulated new approaches and solutions to the problems they found. Reformers used words as weapons in their battles on behalf of children. The documents in this chapter represent the ways in which they tried to alert the public to the perils facing the children in America's cities. The tone of these documents ranges from outraged to sympathetic and from detached to overly optimistic.

CHANGING ATTITUDES TOWARD URBAN CHILDREN, 1872–1909

Attitudes about urban children and assumptions about the proper way to improve their lives changed dramatically between the middle of the nineteenth century and the first decades of the twentieth century. The titles of the books from which the following selections were drawn exemplify these changes. Whereas Charles Loring Brace warned of the "dangerous classes" of New York, Jacob Riis sympathized with the "other half" and Jane Addams celebrated the "spirit of youth."

1

CHARLES LORING BRACE

The Dangerous Classes of New York, and Twenty Years' Work among Them

1872

Charles Loring Brace (1826–1890), a Protestant minister, was the founder of the Children's Aid Society, an agency that removed children from grinding poverty and abuse in the city by sending them to live and work with farm families in upstate New York, the Midwest, or the West. But he had also fought alcoholism, prostitution, and other forms of vice for decades before writing his memoir, and these experiences undoubtedly contributed to his negative attitude toward the urban poor. This excerpt from The Dangerous Classes of New York, and Twenty Years' Work among Them, *published in 1872, describes the threats posed to the rest of society by the poor, dissatisfied, unwashed, and unchurched residents of New York's slums in judgmental, evangelical, and almost defensive terms.*

One of the remarkable and hopeful things about New York, to a close observer of its "dangerous classes," is . . . that they do not tend to become fixed and inherited, as in European cities.

But, though the crime and pauperism of New York are not so deeply stamped in the blood of the population, they are even more dangerous. The intensity of the American temperament is felt in every fibre of these children of poverty and vice. Their crimes have the unrestrained and sanguinary character of a race accustomed to overcome all obstacles. They rifle a bank, where English thieves pick a pocket; they murder, where European *prolétaires* [members of the working class] cudgel or fight with fists; in a riot, they begin what seems about to be the sacking of a city, where English rioters would

Charles Loring Brace, *The Dangerous Classes of New York, and Twenty Years' Work among Them* (New York: Wynkoop & Hallenbeck, 1872), 26–28, 90–93.

merely batter policemen, or smash lamps. The "dangerous classes" of New York are mainly American-born, but the children of Irish and German immigrants. They are as ignorant as London flash-men [professional criminals] or costermongers [hawkers of fruit and vegetables]. They are far more brutal than the peasantry from whom they descend, and they are much banded together, in associations, such as "Dead Rabbit," "Plug-ugly," and various target companies. They are our *enfants perdus* [lost children] grown up to young manhood. The murder of an unoffending old man . . . is nothing to them. They are ready for any offense or crime, however degraded or bloody. New York has never experienced the full effect of the nature of these youthful ruffians as she will one day. They showed their hand only slightly in the riots during the war. At present, they are like the athletes and gladiators of the Roman demagogues. They are the "roughs" who sustain the ward politicians, and frighten honest voters. They can "repeat" [cast more than one vote in local elections] to an unlimited extent, and serve their employers. They live on *"panem et circenses,"*[1] or City-Hall places and pot-houses, where they have full credit.

We shall speak more particularly of the causes of crime in future chapters, but we may say in brief, that the young ruffians of New York are the products of accident, ignorance, and vice. Among a million people, such as compose the population of this city and its suburbs, there will always be a great number of misfortunes; fathers die, and leave their children unprovided for; parents drink, and abuse their little ones, and they float away on the currents of the street; step-mothers or step-fathers drive out, by neglect and ill-treatment, their sons from home. Thousands are the children of poor foreigners, who have permitted them to grow up without school, education, or religion. All the neglect and bad education and evil example of a poor class tend to form others who, as they mature, swell the ranks of ruffians and criminals. So, at length, a great multitude of ignorant, untrained, passionate, irreligious boys and young men are formed, who become the "dangerous classes" of our city. They form the "Nineteenth-street Gangs," the young burglars and murderers, the garroters and rioters, the thieves and flash-men, the "repeaters" and ruffians, so well known to all who know this metropolis. . . .

---

[1] Latin for "bread and circuses," referring to Roman emperors' strategy for keeping the masses happy by providing for their basic needs and offering lavish public entertainments.

The following is the first circular of

THE CHILDREN'S AID SOCIETY

This society has taken its origin in the deeply settled feelings of our citizens, that something must be done to meet the increasing crime and poverty among the destitute children of New York. Its objects are to help this class by opening Sunday Meetings and Industrial Schools, and, gradually as means shall be furnished, by forming Lodging-houses and Reading-rooms for children, and by employing paid agents whose sole business shall be to care for them.

As Christian men, we cannot look upon this great multitude of unhappy, deserted, and degraded boys and girls without feeling our responsibility to God for them. We remember that they have the same capacities, the same need of kind and good influences, and the same Immortality as the little ones in our own homes. We bear in mind that One died for them, even as for the children of the rich and happy. Thus far, alms-houses and prisons have done little to affect the evil. But a small part of the vagrant population can be shut up in our asylums, and judges and magistrates are reluctant to convict children so young and ignorant that they hardly seem able to distinguish good and evil. The class increases. Immigration is pouring in its multitude of poor foreigners, who leave these young outcasts everywhere abandoned in our midst. For the most part, the boys grow up utterly by themselves. No one cares for them, and they care for no one. Some live by begging, by petty pilfering, by bold robbery; some earn an honest support by peddling matches, or apples or newspapers; others gather bones and rags in the street to sell. They sleep on steps, in cellars, in old barns, and in markets, or they hire a bed in filthy and low lodging-houses. They cannot read; they do not go to school or attend a church. Many of them have never seen the Bible. Every cunning faculty is intensely stimulated. They are shrewd and old in vice, when other children are in leading-strings. Few influences which are kind and good ever reach the vagrant boy. And, yet, among themselves they show generous and honest traits. Kindness can always touch them.

The girls, too often, grow up even more pitiable and deserted. Till of late no one has ever cared for them. They are the crosswalk sweepers, the little apple-peddlers, and candy-sellers of our city; or, by more questionable means, they earn their scanty bread. They traverse the low, vile streets alone, and live without mother or friends, or any share in what we should call a *home*. They also know little of God or Christ, except by name. They grow up passionate, ungoverned, with no love or kindness ever to soften the heart. We all know their short wild life—and the sad end.

These boys and girls, it should be remembered, will soon form the great lower class of our city. They will influence elections; they may shape the policy of the city; they will, assuredly, if unreclaimed, poison society all around them. They will help to form the great multitude of robbers, thieves, vagrants, and prostitutes who are now such a burden upon the law-respecting community. . . .

We call upon all who recognize that these are the little ones of Christ; all who believe that crime is best averted by sowing good influences in childhood; all who are the friends of the helpless, to aid us in our enterprise. We confidently hope this wide and practical movement will have its full share of Christian liberality. And we earnestly ask the contributions of those able to give, to help us in carrying forward the work.

2

JACOB RIIS

How the Other Half Lives
1890

Jacob Riis (1849–1914), a Danish immigrant, prowled the slums of New York as a journalist and photographer. No one knew more about the city's mean streets than Riis, and he exposed that awful knowledge in hundreds of photographs and several books. In How the Other Half Lives, *published in 1890, Riis tries to reveal to the wealthier "half" of the population how the poorer "half" lives. As an immigrant himself, and as a passionate critic of the economic and political systems that allowed poor, immigrant neighborhoods to deteriorate and fester, Riis was more interested in exposing the terrible living conditions in the ethnic slums than in blaming the residents for their shortcomings. Readers will notice, however, in this excerpt that he does not hesitate to use simplistic ethnic stereotypes to describe the people he encounters.*

Jacob Riis, *How the Other Half Lives* (New York: Charles Scribner's Sons, 1890, 1901; New York: Dover Publications, 1971), 137–43.

The problem of the children becomes, in these swarms, to the last degree perplexing. Their very number makes one stand aghast. I have already given instances of the packing of the child population in East Side tenements. They might be continued indefinitely until the array would be enough to startle any community. For, be it remembered, these children with the training they receive—or do not receive— with the instincts they inherit and absorb in their growing up, are to be our future rulers, if our theory of government is worth anything. More than a working majority of our voters now register from the tenements. I counted the other day the little ones, up to ten years or so, in a Bayard Street tenement that for a yard has a triangular space in the centre with sides fourteen or fifteen feet long, just room enough for a row of ill-smelling closets [outhouses] at the base of the triangle and a hydrant [for water for domestic use] at the apex. There was about as much light in this "yard" as in the average cellar. I gave up my self-imposed task in despair when I had counted one hundred and twenty-eight in forty families. Thirteen I had missed, or not found in. Applying the average for the forty to the whole fifty-three, the house contained one hundred and seventy children. It is not the only time I have had to give up such census work. I have in mind an alley—an inlet rather to a row of rear tenements—that is either two or four feet wide according as the wall of the crazy old building that gives on it bulges out or in. I tried to count the children that swarmed there, but could not. Sometimes I have doubted that anybody knows just how many there are about. Bodies of drowned children turn up in the rivers right along in summer whom no one seems to know anything about. When last spring some workmen, while moving a pile of lumber on a North River pier, found under the last plank the body of a little lad crushed to death, no one had missed a boy, though his parents afterward turned up. The truant officer assuredly does not know, though he spends his life trying to find out, somewhat illogically, perhaps since the department that employs him admits that thousands of poor children are crowded out of the schools year by year for want of room. There was a big tenement in the Sixth Ward, now happily appropriated by the beneficent spirit of business that blots out so many foul spots in New York—it figured not long ago in the official reports as "an out-and-out hogpen"—that had a record of one hundred and two arrests in four years among its four hundred and seventy-eight tenants, fifty-seven of them for drunken and disorderly conduct. I do not know how many children there were in it, but the inspector reported that he found only seven in the whole house who owned that they went to school. The rest gathered all the instruction they received running for beer for their elders. Some of them claimed the "flat" as their home as a mere matter of form. They slept in the streets at night. The official came upon a little party of four drinking beer out of the cover of a milk-can in the hallway. They were of the seven good boys and proved their claim to the title by offering him some.

The old question, what to do with the boy, assumes a new and serious phase in the tenement. Under the best conditions found there, it is not easily answered. In nine cases out of ten he would make an excellent mechanic, if trained early to work at a trade, for he is neither dull nor slow, but the short-sighted despotism of the trades unions has practically closed that avenue to him. Trade-schools, however excellent, cannot supply the opportunity thus denied him, and at the outset the boy stands condemned by his own to low and ill-paid drudgery, held down by the hand that of all should labor to raise him. Home, the greatest factor of all in the training of the young, means nothing to him but a pigeon-hole in a coop along with so many other human animals. Its influence is scarcely of the elevating kind, if it have any. The very games at which he takes a hand in the street become polluting in its atmosphere. With no steady hand to guide him, the boy takes naturally to idle ways. Caught in the street by the truant officer, or by agents of the Children's Societies, peddling, perhaps, or begging, to help out the family resources, he runs the risk of being sent to a reformatory, where contact with vicious boys older than himself soon develop the latent possibilities for evil that lie hidden in him. The city has no Truant Home in which to keep him, and all efforts of the children's friends to enforce school attendance are paralyzed by this want. The risk of the reformatory is too great. What is done in the end is to let him take chances—with the chances all against him. The result is the rough young savage, familiar from the street. Rough as he is, if any one doubt that this child of common clay have in him the instinct of beauty, of love for the ideal of which his life has no embodiment, let him put the matter to the test. Let him take into a tenement block a handful of flowers from the fields and watch the brightened faces, the sudden abandonment of play and fight that go ever hand in hand where there is no elbow-room, the wild entreaty for "posies," the eager love with which the little messengers of peace are shielded, once possessed; then let him change his mind. I have seen an armful of daisies keep the peace of a block better than a policeman and his club, seen instincts awaken under their gentle appeal, whose very existence the soil in which they grew made seem a mockery. I have not forgotten the deputation of ragamuffins from a Mulberry Street alley that knocked at my office door one morning on a mysterious expedition for flowers, not for themselves, but for "a lady," and having obtained what they wanted, trooped off to bestow them, a ragged and dirty little band, with a solemnity that was quite unusual. It was not until an old man called the next day to thank me for the flowers that I found out they had decked the bier of a pauper, in the dark rear room where she lay waiting in her pine-board coffin for the city's hearse. Yet, as I knew, that dismal alley with its bare brick walls, between which no sun ever rose or set, was the world of those children. It filled their young lives. Probably not one of them had ever been out of the sight of it. They were too dirty, too ragged, and too generally disreputable, too well hidden in their slum besides, to come into line with the Fresh Air summer boarders.

With such human instincts and cravings, forever unsatisfied, turned into a haunting curse; with appetite ground to keenest edge by a hunger that is never fed, the children of the poor grow up in joyless homes to lives of wearisome toil that claims them at an age when the play of their happier fellows has but just begun. Has a yard of turf been laid and a vine been coaxed to grow within their reach, they are banished and barred out from it as from a heaven that is not for such as they. I came upon a couple of youngsters in a Mulberry Street yard a while ago that were chalking on the fence their first lesson in "writin'." And this is what they wrote: "Keeb of te Grass." They had it by heart, for there was not, I verily believe, a green sod within a quarter of a mile. Home to them is an empty name. Pleasure? A gentleman once catechized a ragged class in a down-town public school on this point, and recorded the result: Out of forty-eight boys twenty had never seen the Brooklyn Bridge that was scarcely five minutes' walk away, three only had been in Central Park, fifteen had known the joy of a ride in a horse-car. The street, with its ash-barrels and its dirt, the river that runs foul with mud, are their domain. What training they receive is picked up there. And they are apt pupils. If the mud and the dirt are easily reflected in their lives, what wonder? Scarce half-grown, such lads as these confront the world with the challenge to give them their due, too long withheld, or——. Our jails supply the answer to the alternative.

A little fellow who seemed clad in but a single rag was among the flotsam and jetsam stranded at Police Headquarters one day last summer. No one knew where he came from or where he belonged. The boy himself knew as little about it as anybody, and was the least anxious to have light shed on the subject after he had spent a night in the matron's nursery. The discovery that beds were provided for boys to sleep in there, and that he could have "a whole egg" and three slices of bread for breakfast put him on the best of terms with the world in general, and he decided that Headquarters was "a bully place." He sang "McGinty" all through, with Tenth Avenue variations, for the police, and then settled down to the serious business of giving an account of himself. The examination went on after this fashion:

"Where do you go to church, my boy?"

"We don't have no clothes to go to church." And indeed his appearance, as he was, in the door of any New York church would have caused a sensation.

"Well, where do you go to school, then?"

"I don't go to school," with a snort of contempt.

"Where do you buy your bread?"

"We don't buy no bread; we buy beer," said the boy, and it was eventually the saloon that led the police as a landmark to his "home." It was worthy of the boy. As he had said, his only bed was a heap of dirty straw on the floor, his daily diet a crust in the morning, nothing else.

Into the rooms of the Children's Aid Society were led two little girls whose father had "busted up the house" and put them on the street after their mother died. Another, who was turned out by her stepmother "because she had five of her own and could not afford to keep her," could not remember ever having been in church or Sunday-school, and only knew the name of Jesus through hearing people swear by it. She had no idea what they meant. These were specimens of the overflow from the tenements of our home-heathen that are growing up in New York's streets to-day, while tender hearted men and women are busying themselves with the socks and the hereafter of well-fed little Hottentots thousands of miles away. According to Canon Taylor, of York, one hundred and nine missionaries in the four fields of Persia, Palestine, Arabia, and Egypt spent one year and sixty thousand dollars in converting one little heathen girl. If there is nothing the matter with those missionaries, they might come to New York with a good deal better prospect of success.

By those who lay flattering unction to their souls in the knowledge that to-day New York has, at all events, no brood of the gutters of tender years that can be homeless long unheeded, let it be remembered well through what effort this judgment has been averted. In thirty-seven years the Children's Aid Society, that came into existence as an emphatic protest against the tenement corruption of the young, has sheltered quite three hundred thousand outcast, homeless, and orphaned children in its lodging-houses, and has found homes in the West for seventy thousand that had none. Doubtless, as a mere stroke of finance, the five millions and a half thus spent were a wiser investment than to have let them grow up thieves and thugs. In the last fifteen years of this tireless battle for the safety of the State the intervention of the Society for the Prevention of Cruelty to Children has been invoked for 138,891 little ones; it has thrown its protection around more than twenty-five thousand helpless children, and has convicted nearly sixteen thousand wretches of child-beating and abuse. Add to this the standing army of fifteen thousand dependent children in New York's asylums and institutions, and some idea is gained of the crop that is garnered day by day in the tenements, of the enormous force employed to check their inroads on our social life, and of the cause for apprehension that would exist did their efforts flag for ever so brief a time.

Nothing is now better understood than that the rescue of the children is the key to the problem of city poverty, as presented for our solution to-day; that a character may be formed where to reform it would be a hopeless task. The concurrent testimony of all who have to undertake it at a later stage: that the young are naturally neither vicious nor hardened, simply weak and undeveloped, except by the bad influences of the street, makes this duty all the more urgent as well as hopeful. Helping hands are held out on every side. To private charity the municipality leaves the entire care of its proletariat of tender years, lulling its conscience to sleep with liberal appropriations of money to foot the bills. Indeed, it is held by those whose opinions are entitled to weight that it is far too liberal a paymaster for its own best interests and those of its wards. It deals with the evil in the seed to a limited extent in gathering in the outcast babies from the streets. To the ripe fruit the gates of its prisons, its reformatories, and its workhouses are opened wide the year round. What the showing would be at this end of the line were it not for the barriers wise charity has thrown across the broad highway to ruin—is building day by day—may be measured by such results as those quoted above in the span of a single life.

3

JANE ADDAMS

The Spirit of Youth and the City Streets

1909

Jane Addams (1860–1935) was a contemporary of Riis's, but as the cofounder (with Ellen Gates Starr) of Hull House, the famous Chicago settlement house, and as a member of the Chicago school board, one of the founders of the National Association for the Advancement of Colored People (NAACP), and a leader in the women's suffrage and international peace movements, she was more interested in finding solutions than in casting blame. The staff at Hull House, for instance, offered courses in citizenship; taught classes in English, housekeeping, and nutrition; organized kindergartens and summer camps; and helped the unemployed find jobs. Addams's faith in the benefits of belonging to a small community—even in the middle of a metropolis—recalls her small-town girlhood and shows a positive side of city life absent from the writings of Brace and Riis.

Nothing is more certain than that each generation longs for a reassurance as to the value and charm of life, and is secretly afraid lest it lose its sense of the youth of the earth. This is doubtless one reason why it so passionately cherishes its poets and artists who have been able to explore for themselves and to reveal to others the perpetual springs of life's self-renewal.

And yet the average man cannot obtain this desired reassurance through literature, nor yet through glimpses of earth and sky. It can come to him only through the chance embodiment of joy and youth which life itself may throw in his way. It is doubtless true that for the mass of men the message is never so unchallenged and so invincible as when embodied in youth itself. One generation after another has depended upon its young to equip it with gaiety and enthusiasm, to persuade it that living is a pleasure, until men everywhere have anxiously provided channels through which this wine of life might flow, and be

Jane Addams, *The Spirit of Youth and the City Streets* (New York: Macmillan Company, 1909; Urbana: University of Illinois Press, 1972), 3–9, 13–16.

39

preserved for their delight. The classical city promoted play with careful solicitude, building the theater and stadium as it built the market place and the temple. The Greeks held their games so integral a part of religion and patriotism that they came to expect from their poets the highest utterances at the very moments when the sense of pleasure released the national life. In the medieval city the knights held their tourneys, the guilds their pageants, the people their dances, and the church made festival for its most cherished saints with gay street processions, and presented a drama in which no less a theme than the history of creation became a matter of thrilling interest. Only in the modern city have men concluded that it is no longer necessary for the municipality to provide for the insatiable desire for play. In so far as they have acted upon this conclusion, they have entered upon a most difficult and dangerous experiment; and this at the very moment when the city has become distinctly industrial, and daily labor is continually more monotonous and subdivided. We forget how new the modern city is, and how short the span of time in which we have assumed that we can eliminate public provision for recreation.

A further difficulty lies in the fact that this industrialism has gathered together multitudes of eager young creatures from all quarters of the earth as a labor supply for the countless factories and workshops, upon which the present industrial city is based. Never before in civilization have such numbers of young girls been suddenly released from the protection of the home and permitted to walk unattended upon city streets and to work under alien roofs; for the first time they are being prized more for their labor power than for their innocence, their tender beauty, their ephemeral gaiety. Society cares more for the products they manufacture than for their immemorial ability to reaffirm the charm of existence. Never before have such numbers of young boys earned money independently of the family life, and felt themselves free to spend it as they choose in the midst of vice deliberately disguised as pleasure.

This stupid experiment of organizing work and failing to organize play has, of course, brought about a fine revenge. The love of pleasure will not be denied, and when it has turned into all sorts of malignant and vicious appetites, then we, the middle aged, grow quite distracted and resort to all sorts of restrictive measures. We even try to dam up the sweet fountain itself because we are affrighted by these neglected streams; but almost worse than the restrictive measures is our apparent belief that the city itself has no obligation in the matter, an assumption upon which the modern city turns over to commercialism practically all the provisions for public recreation.

Quite as one set of men has organized the young people into indus-trial enterprises in order to profit from their toil, so another set of men and also of women, I am sorry to say, have entered the neglected field of recreation and have organized enterprises which make profit out of this invincible love of pleasure.

In every city arise so-called "places"—"gin-palaces," they are called in fiction; in Chicago we euphemistically say merely "places,"—in which alcohol is dispensed, not to allay thirst, but, ostensibly to stimu-late gaiety, it is sold really in order to empty pockets. Huge dance halls are opened to which hundreds of young people are attracted, many of whom stand wistfully outside a roped circle, for it requires five cents to procure within it for five minutes the sense of allurement and intoxication which is sold in lieu of innocent pleasure. These coarse and illicit merrymakings remind one of the unrestrained jolli-ties of Restoration London, and they are indeed their direct descen-dants, properly commercialized, still confusing joy with lust, and gaiety with debauchery. Since the soldiers of Cromwell[1] shut up the people's playhouses and destroyed their pleasure fields, the Anglo-Saxon city has turned over the provision for public recreation to the most evil-minded and the most unscrupulous members of the commu-nity. We see thousands of girls walking up and down the streets on a pleasant evening with no chance to catch a sight of pleasure even through a lighted window, save as these lurid places provide it. Appar-ently the modern city sees in these girls only two possibilities, both of them commercial: first, a chance to utilize by day their new and tender labor power in its factories and shops, and then another chance in the evening to extract from them their petty wages by pandering to their love of pleasure.

As these overworked girls stream along the street, the rest of us see only the self-conscious walk, the giggling speech, the preposter-ous clothing. And yet through the huge hat, with its wilderness of bedraggled feathers, the girl announces to the world that she is here. She demands attention to the fact of her existence, she states that she is ready to live, to take her place in the world. The most precious moment in human development is the young creature's assertion that he is unlike any other human being, and has an individual contribu-tion to make to the world. The variation from the established type is at the root of all change, the only possible basis for progress, all that keeps life from growing unprofitably stale and repetitious. . . .

[1]Oliver Cromwell led the victorious Puritan forces in the English civil war of the 1640s.

Perhaps never before have the pleasures of the young and mature become so definitely separated as in the modern city. The public dance halls filled with frivolous and irresponsible young people in a feverish search for pleasure, are but a sorry substitute for the old dances on the village green in which all of the older people of the village participated. Chaperonage was not then a social duty but natural and inevitable, and the whole courtship period was guarded by the conventions and restraint which were taken as a matter of course and had developed through years of publicity and simple propriety.

The only marvel is that the stupid attempt to put the fine old wine of traditional country life into the new bottles of the modern town does not lead to disaster oftener than it does, and that the wine so long remains pure and sparkling.

We cannot afford to be ungenerous to the city in which we live without suffering the penalty which lack of fair interpretation always entails. Let us know the modern city in its weakness and wickedness, and then seek to rectify and purify it until it shall be free at least from the grosser temptations which now beset the young people who are living in its tenement houses and working in its factories. The mass of these young people are possessed of good intentions and they are equipped with a certain understanding of city life. This itself could be made a most valuable social instrument toward securing innocent recreation and better social organization. They are already serving the city in so far as it is honey-combed with mutual benefit societies, with "pleasure clubs," with organizations connected with churches and factories which are filling a genuine social need. And yet the whole apparatus for supplying pleasure is wretchedly inadequate and full of danger to whomsoever may approach it. Who is responsible for its inadequacy and dangers? We certainly cannot expect the fathers and mothers who have come to the city from farms or who have emigrated from other lands to appreciate or rectify these dangers. We cannot expect the young people themselves to cling to conventions which are totally unsuited to modern city conditions, nor yet to be equal to the task of forming new conventions through which this more agglomerate social life may express itself. Above all we cannot hope that they will understand the emotional force which seizes them and which, when it does not find the traditional line of domesticity, serves as a cancer in the very tissues of society and as a disrupter of the securest social bonds. No attempt is made to treat the manifestations of this fundamental instinct with dignity or to give it possible social utility. The spontaneous joy, the clamor for pleasure, the desire of the young people to appear finer and better and altogether more lovely than they really are, the idealization not only of each other but of the whole earth which they regard but as a theater for their noble exploits, the unworldly ambitions, the romantic hopes, the make-believe world in which they live, if properly utilized, what might they not do to make our sordid cities more beautiful, more companionable?

STUDIES OF CITY BOYS AND GIRLS

Reformers in the Progressive Era insisted that the first step in solving social problems was to measure the magnitude of those problems. As a result, numerous studies of children's work, schooling, and leisure activities were conducted by government agencies, private organizations, and individuals. These studies—including the three excerpted below—employed typical Progressive methodologies: surveys; interviews with youths, parents, social workers, police officers, and government officials; and reports by researchers trained to observe the activities being investigated. In addition to representing typical methods for researching children's lives, the results provide slices of girls' and boys' lives early in the twentieth century. Although most of the studies reflect the thoughts of adults, from time to time the voices of children and youth break through the reformers' rhetoric.

4

VICE COMMISSION OF THE CITY OF CHICAGO

The Social Evil in Chicago: Study of Existing Conditions with Recommendations

1911

In 1911 the Chicago Vice Commission published a major study on the "social evil": prostitution. The study described the conditions that encouraged girls and women to become prostitutes; the poorly regulated dance halls, clubs, and tenements that allowed the practice to flourish; and the

Vice Commission of the City of Chicago, *The Social Evil in Chicago: Study of Existing Conditions with Recommendations* (Chicago: Vice Commission of the City of Chicago, 1911), 35–37, 38–39, 174–75.

legal, political, and social institutions that had failed to suppress it. An undercurrent throughout the study is the concern about the sexual exploitation of teenage girls — often called "white slavery" — which a year earlier had led the U.S. Congress to pass the Mann Act outlawing the transportation across state lines of any woman or girl in order to commit "immoral acts."

PROTECTION OF CHILDREN

We often forget that society owes much to the protection of the children. Those of mature years can be left generally to guard themselves; but in the case of youth and ignorance, society must take the part of the elder brother, and in many cases, the part of the father as an educator and guardian.

From its study of existing conditions in Chicago the Commission feels that if there is to be any permanent gain in the fight against the Social Evil in this city, much care and thought must be given the problem of child protection and education. . . . [T]he children in certain sections of the city are surrounded by many immoral influences and dangers. They are compelled by reason of poverty to live within, or in close proximity to, restricted prostitute districts. Even in residential sections children come in contact with immoral persons, and gain an early knowledge of things which may influence their whole life and guide them in the wrong direction.

One of the sad spectacles in this great city is the night children who sell gum, candy, and papers on the streets. These little vendors become creatures of independent habits before they reach the age of puberty. Through habits learned by loitering near saloons, and even in the rear rooms frequented by prostitutes and vile men, they become familiar with the vulgarity and immorality of the street and learn their language and ways of life. All of this knowledge, far beyond their years, results in defiance on the part of these children against parental will and authority. That children should be kept off the streets at night by the police, and that parents should be impressed with the importance of the most strict supervision of the child's recreational hours, are two matters of the greatest moment in the protection of the child.

The investigations by the Commission show that messengers and newsboys have an intimate knowledge of the ways of the underworld. Their moral sense is so blunted as to be absolutely blind to the degredation of women and the vile influence of vicious men. Thus early in life they become diseased both in body and soul and grow up to enter upon a career of crime and lust.

Much good is being accomplished by various philanthropic organizations, particularly the Juvenile Protective Association, in calling the public attention to these grave dangers, and caring for children who are victims of such environments.

The Commission heartily endorses all attempts to provide healthful and carefully guarded places of recreation for the children. It does not sympathize with those who simply stand by to criticize without doing anything in a constructive way to provide something wholesome for that which may demoralize. Children must and should have amusement and recreation, and they will find it in some way. Let Chicago increase her small parks and recreation centers. Let the churches give of their facilities to provide amusement for children. Let the Board of Education extend its efforts in establishing more social centers in the public schools. Let the city provide clean dances, well chaperoned— as they are now in the public schools' Social Centers.

SEX EDUCATION

Many of the immoral influences and dangers which are constantly surrounding young children on the street, in their amusements, and in business life, may be counteracted and minimized by proper moral teaching and scientific instruction. Educators have come to feel something should be done directly by teachers in schools and elsewhere to impart some kind of instruction to counteract the evil knowledge which children acquire from evil sources.

The Commission believes that in the case of children beyond the age of puberty sex hygiene may be taught in schools under carefully trained and scientifically instructed teachers. For younger children the parents should do the teaching as the part of a sacred duty. In the case of the father being unwilling to do so, let the family physician be asked to teach the son. The mother, with her maternal instinct, will find the way and means to warn the daughter of the dangers which may beset her. In colleges and universities sex hygiene should be universally taught. The Commission feels that the teaching of sex hygiene in schools is an important movement which, while not yet past the experimental stage, promises great advances in the promotion of child protection for the future. But it is certain that knowledge of sex hygiene alone can never be successful in saving the child until it is based upon religious conviction and sound moral training.

The lack of home instruction in the use and abuse of sex organs and relationship leads many children to a knowledge gained in sad ways with unhappy results. Fortunate, indeed, is the boy or girl, who has a father or mother as a confidant with whom there may be free conversation concerning the natural functions of the body—a conversation raised almost to a point of spirituality because of the parent's pure love for the child, and the child's unfaltering trust in the parent. If more fathers and mothers could be companions and comrades with their children there would be far less need of Commissions of this kind to solve perplexing problems for the parents.

We record our conviction that while intelligence regarding sexual matters, if dictated by moral sentiment, is a safeguard to the youth of the community, yet the indiscriminate circulation of sexual information among children by means of books and pamphlets suggests a danger which ought not to escape attention. These publications are of two sorts. The first includes the vicious prints which even assume the guise of helpful instruction to accomplish their purpose. The second comprises those works on sexual science which, with the best intent, are prepared for the use of children. We are firmly of the opinion that such material should be used by parents and other instructors of the children in securing information which they may impart to those in their care, rather than by the children themselves in whose hands it is liable to awaken morbid curiosity and to result in harm. . . .

THE SITUATION IN COLORED COMMUNITIES

The history of the social evil in Chicago is intimately connected with the colored population. Invariably the larger vice districts have been created within or near the settlements of colored people. In the past history of the city, nearly every time a new vice district was created down town or on the South Side, the colored families were in the district, moving in just ahead of the prostitutes. The situation along State street from 16th street south is an illustration.

So whenever prostitutes, cadets [pimps], and thugs were located among white people and had to be moved for commercial or other reasons, they were driven to undesirable parts of the city, the so-called colored residential sections. A former Chief of Police gave out a semi-official statement to the effect that so long as this degenerate group of persons confined their residence to districts west of Wabash avenue and east of Wentworth avenue they would not be apprehended. This part of the city is the largest residence section of colored families. Their churches, Sunday schools and societies, are within these boundaries. In this colored community there is a large number of disorderly saloons, gambling houses, assignation rooms and houses of ill-fame. An investigation shows that there are several thousand colored people in the First, Second, and Third Wards where these vicious conditions obtain. Under these conditions in the Second and Third Wards there are 1,475 young colored boys and girls.

In addition to this proximity to immoral conditions young colored girls are often forced into idleness because of a prejudice against them, and they are eventually forced to accept positions as maids in houses of prostitution.

Employment agents do not hesitate to send colored girls as servants to these houses. They make the astounding statement that the law does not allow them to send white girls but they will furnish colored help!

In summing up it is an appalling fact that practically all of the male and female servants connected with houses of prostitution in vice districts and in disorderly flats in residential sections are colored. The majority of entertainers in disorderly saloons on the South Side are colored men who live with, and in part upon, the proceeds of white women.

The apparent discrimination against the colored citizens of the city in permitting vice to be set down in their very midst is unjust, and abhorrent to all fair minded people. Colored children should receive the same moral protection that white children receive.

The prejudice against colored girls who are ambitious to earn an honest living is unjust. Such an attitude eventually drives them into immoral surroundings. They need special care and protection on the maxim that it is the duty of the strong to help the weak. Any effort, therefore, to improve conditions in Chicago should provide more wholesome surroundings for the families of its colored citizens who now live in communities of colored people.

PERVERSION

At the very outset of the Commission's investigation its attention was called by several persons to the practice of sexual perversion which was said to be very prevalent and growing in Chicago. The investigation of the Commission bears out this assertion.

It must be understood that the perpetrators of these various forms of sexual perversion can be regarded as those who may be punished under the law relating to infamous crimes. . . .

Analysis of Data from Juvenile Court Records

The records of 2,241 young girls brought before the Juvenile Court of Chicago during the first ten years of its operation, charged with immorality, or other offenses involving sexual irregularity. The cases of all these girls were carefully investigated by the Department of Social Investigation of the Chicago School of Civics and Philanthropy, in preparing a report on the Juvenile Court of Cook County for the Russell Sage Foundation, soon to be published in two volumes. The cases of these girls were patiently and carefully examined, not only as they appear upon the records of the court, but by personal inquiry of several hundreds of these girls themselves, their parents, and others acquainted with their history.

The offenses for which they were brought into court were as follows: On the charge of being disorderly or incorrigible, 1,370; and on the direct charge of immorality, 871. It should be understood that the word "immoral" is never used in the petition or statement of the case, if it can be avoided. The offenses disguised in the court records under the terms "incorrigibility" or "disorderly conduct" involve in a large percentage of cases sexual irregularity. This percentage is estimated from 65 to 80 per cent of all these 2,241 young girls, arraigned before the Juvenile Court as delinquents. This fact is more significant in view of their youth, since only 15 per cent of them are over sixteen years of age, and nearly half of them are fourteen years, or younger.

The degraded condition in the homes from which many of these girls came is pitifully apparent. Among 168 girls committed to the State Training School from Chicago, 30 had intemperate fathers, 8 intemperate mothers, 20 had fathers who were of vicious habits, 16 were children of immoral, vicious, or criminal mothers, while in the families of 12 there were others than the parents who had vicious or criminal records. In 24 cases the father had shirked all responsibility and deserted the family. Eleven of these girls were illegitimate children, or had been abandoned, and 10 had been victims of gross cruelty, 29 had been in houses of prostitution, or had been promiscuously immoral, one having been a "common street walker" at eleven years of age. Thirteen had sisters who had become immoral, and had been committed to public institutions on that account. Fourteen had brothers who had been in such institutions for the care of delinquent boys and men.

Among the girls committed from other sections of the State, 31 allege that the companion of their first experience in sexual irregularity was a member of their own family, and 16 Chicago girls had the same experience. *In* 19 *cases it was the father,* in 5 the uncle, in 8 the brother or older cousin who had wronged the child; in 72 other cases, girls brought in as delinquents before the Juvenile Court had been wronged in this way, 32 *by their own fathers.* In 189 other cases in which the girls were charged with immorality, the mother or the legal guardian was implicated in the offense, if not responsible for it. In 18 cases, the delinquent girls were children of common prostitutes, in 23 cases their mothers were known to be immoral, though not "professionally." In 74 other cases, the mother was described as "of questionable morals" or "of doubtful character," and in 51 cases the mother was intemperate. We are thus confronted by a total of 346 cases, in which the court records show that the guardian under whose care the girl was growing up was obviously unfit to be trusted with the care of a young girl.

5

CHICAGO COMMISSION ON RACE RELATIONS

The Negro in Chicago: A Study of Race Relations and a Race Riot

1922

Race relations may have played a minor role in the findings of the Vice Commission, but they were at the center of The Negro in Chicago, *an analysis of the causes of the city's 1919 race riot, which killed thirty-eight people and injured nearly three hundred. In seeking to understand the origins of racial tensions, researchers for the Chicago Commission on Race Relations studied the relationships between white and African American students in the city's elementary and high schools. The study reveals a burgeoning youth culture in the city's schools, as white and African American youngsters participate in numerous extracurricular and social activities. (The parenthetical information refers to the names of the schools or to the percentage of black students in specific schools.)*

The Chicago Commission on Race Relations, *The Negro in Chicago: A Study of Race Relations and a Race Riot* (Chicago: University of Chicago Press, 1922), 246–50, 252–55.

1. Elementary Schools

The contacts in the elementary schools fall naturally under three heads: classroom contacts, building and playground contacts, and social contacts.

CLASSROOM CONTACTS

There was much less variety of opinion in regard to classroom contacts than the other two. Most teachers agreed that there was little friction so far as school work was concerned, even when it meant sitting next to one another or in the same seats. Most kindergarten teachers found the most natural relationship existing between the young Negro and white children. "Neither colored nor whites have any feeling in our kindergarten," said one principal in a school 30 per cent Negro (Webster); "they don't understand the difference between colored and white children." In visiting one school the investigator noticed that the white children who objected to holding hands with the Negro children in the kindergarten and first and second grades were the better-dressed children who undoubtedly reflected the economic class and race consciousness of their parents. The Armour Mission near the school had excluded Negroes from its kindergarten, thereby fostering this spirit among the whites. A teacher in Doolittle (85 per cent) told of a little white girl in another school who cried because she was afraid the color from the Negro children's hands would rub off on hers; in her present school she has known no such instances in the kindergarten. This conduct is paralleled in instances in which Negro children who have never had any contact with white children in the South are afraid of them when they first come North.

Most of the teachers in the higher grades reported that there were no signs of race prejudice in the room. A teacher at Oakland (26 per cent) said that white girls sometimes asked to be moved to another seat when near a very dirty Negro child, but that this often happened when the dirty child was white. This teacher said it was the white mothers from the South, not the children, who wanted their children to be kept away from the Negroes. "The white children don't seem to mind the colored," she said. "I have had three or four mothers come in and ask that their children be kept away from the colored, but they were women from the South and felt race prejudice strongly. But they are the only ones who have complained."

A teacher in a school 90 per cent Negro said that when doubling up in the seats was necessary whites and Negroes frequently chose each other. A teacher at Moseley (70 per cent), when the investigator was present, called upon a white girl to act as hostess to a Negro girl who had just come from the South, and the request was met with pride and pleasure by the white girl. On the same occasion a white boy was asked to help a Negro boy with his arithmetic, and the two doubled up and worked together quite naturally.

"Race makes no difference," declared the principal of a school 92 per cent Negro (Colman). "The other day I had them all digging in the garden, and when they were all ready to go in I kept out one colored boy to help me plant seeds. We could use another boy, so I told Henry to choose anyone out of two rooms and he returned with an Italian. The color makes no difference."

A few instances of jealousy are cited. In one of them resentment ran high because when a loving cup was presented in McKinley (70 per cent) for the best composition, it was awarded by a neutral outside jury to a white girl. The principal of this 70 per cent Negro school, in addition to finding the Negro children jealous, considered their parents insolent and resentful. On the investigator's first visit she said that military discipline was the only kind for children, and that absolute segregation was necessary. At the next interview she said she preferred her school to any other; that there was never any disciplinary difficulty, and that white children who had moved from the district were paying car fare to finish their course at her school.

DISCIPLINE

There was considerable variety of opinion among the teachers as to whether Negro children presented any special problems of discipline. The principal of a school 20 per cent Negro (Felsenthal), for example, said that discipline was more difficult in this school than in the branch where 90 per cent were Negroes (Fuller). This principal is an advocate of separate schools. She was contradicted by a teacher in her school who said she had never used different discipline for the Negroes. In schools where the principals were sympathetic and the interracial spirit good the teachers reported that Negro children were much like other children and could be disciplined in the same way. One or two teachers reported that Negro children could not be scolded but must be "jollied along" and the work presented as play. This is interesting in view of the frequent complaint of the children from the South that the teachers in Chicago played with them all the time and did not teach them anything.

ATTITUDE TOWARD NEGRO TEACHERS

Few Negro teachers were found in the schools investigated.

At Doolittle (85 per cent) there were thirty-three teachers, of whom two were Negroes. There was also a Negro cadet. At Raymond (93 per cent) there were six Negro teachers and a Negro cadet in a staff of forty. At Keith (90 per cent) there were six Negro teachers in a staff of twelve. Two of these principals said that their Negro teachers compared favorably with their white teachers and that some of them were excellent. Asked whether there was much antagonism if a Negro teacher was assigned where all the children were white, the principal of a 93 per cent school (Raymond) said there had been one or two such cases. "They are most successful in the foreign districts on the West Side. The European people do not seem to resent the presence of a colored teacher."

Another principal said that this was especially true where the foreign element was Jewish. A Negro teacher in a West Side school, largely Italian, is considered one of the ablest teachers in the school and proved herself highly competent during the war, when she assisted with the work of the draft board in the district.

One or two principals said that they would not have Negro teachers in their schools because the white teachers "could not be intimate with colored teachers," or because Negro teachers were "cocky," or because "the *Defender*[1] preaches propaganda for colored teachers to seek positions in white schools." Sometimes an effort was made to explain the principal's objection to Negro teachers by saying that Negro children had no respect for Negro teachers. One principal whose white teachers were rather below the accepted standard said that the one colored teacher who had been there was obliged to leave because of the children's protest against her. A Negro teacher in a 20 percent school (Haven) was valued highly by the principal, who advised with her as to what measures could be taken to prevent the appearance of race feeling. This teacher formerly taught in a school where there were no Negro children and had experienced no difficulty in either type of school. "The children just seem to forget I am colored," she said.

In Farren School (92 per cent) a teacher of a special room for chil-

---

[1]The *Chicago Defender* was the leading African American newspaper in the United States.

dren recently arrived from the South expressed the belief that these children "have a distinct and decided fear of the white teacher and it's up to the teacher to change this fear into respect." They were very timid at first, she said, due to the new environment and the contact with so many more people, especially white. This timidity lasted for about a year and then these children became more like Chicago children.

BUILDING AND PLAYGROUND CONTACTS

At six out of the thirteen elementary schools some friction about the buildings and on the playgrounds was reported, and none at the other seven schools. On further analysis it appeared that the friction reported was general at only two of the six schools. At the other four the instances cited seemed either to involve a few troublesome individuals or to be quarrels among Negro children rather than between Negroes and whites. The two schools reporting general antagonism between Negro and white children had about 30 per cent Negro children. The principals of these schools said that the white children were dominated by the Negroes and did not dare stand up for their rights. The testimony of the principal of one of these schools showed a disposition to regard many acts as characteristically racial. For example, she needed no further evidence that a Negro boy had cut up a white boy's cap than the fact that it was cut with a safety-razor blade. Although both white and Negro boys commonly carry safety-razor blades to sharpen their pencils, she thought of razors only in connection with Negroes. She also believed that "Negro children of kindergarten age are unusually cruel," and that "Negroes need a curriculum especially adapted to their emotional natures." Again she said that a Negro boy who asked to be put back from the third to the first grade, because the third-grade work was too hard for him, was typical of Negro children, who "shut down on their intellectual processes when they are about twelve or fourteen years of age." In view of the numbers of Negro children in the higher grades who are advancing normally, this is obviously an unwarranted generalization.

There were some signs of friction at a school 20 per cent Negro (Haven) when a school largely Italian was combined with it, but the situation was handled tactfully by the principal and there had been no trouble. At a school 85 per cent Negro (Doolittle), where the white element was Jewish, all the teachers reported that there was no antagonism between the races.

VOLUNTARY GROUPING

The only school where the investigator noticed Negro and white children playing in separate groups was Webster (30 per cent), whose principal reported antagonism between Negroes and whites. At the other schools natural mingling was reported by some teachers or observed by the investigator. At a school 26 per cent Negro (Oakland) three teachers said that Negro and white children did not mingle on the playgrounds, while another teacher said they all played together regardless of color. The principal and twelve teachers at a school 85 per cent Negro (Doolittle) agreed, with the exception of one teacher who was a southerner, that there was never anything but the most natural mingling in the classrooms, about the building and on the playground. At a school 30 per cent Negro (Drake), the principal of which stated that the relations between the races were not harmonious, the investigator observed a free and natural grouping of Negroes and whites of all ages on the playground. The principal explained that this was "a forced rather than a natural grouping because of lack of apparatus for all." The white children at a school 20 per cent Negro (Haven) were Italians, Jews, and Greeks, and all the races played so naturally together that passersby frequently stopped to watch them.

SOCIAL CONTACTS

There are few social organizations and gatherings in the elementary schools. The principal of a school 93 percent Negro (Raymond) said that there were clubs through all the grammar grades and that the friendliness between the two races was marked, but added:

> We have not more than fifty or sixty white children in this particular building. One white child was elected vice-president, the first white child elected in eight years. It shows the friendly relationship when a white child could be elected to office with a large preponderance of colored children. A Jewish boy was elected to a smaller office of clerk. The white children are not foreign. In their meetings the question of color never arises at all.

In a few instances principals had found that graduation presented some difficulties, as white mothers would appear at the school a few days before and request that their children do not march with Negro children. "About the only time I see a white mother is near graduation," said the principal of a school 38 per cent Negro (Forrestville). "They always say they wouldn't care for themselves, but a friend might see and they would feel ashamed." "White children prefer not to march with colored at graduation," said a teacher at Oakland School (26 per cent), "and mothers sometimes come to ask that it be so arranged that their girls can march with white girls. They usually say that for themselves they don't mind, but friends might see and wonder why that should be."

A number of the schools have orchestras or occasional musical programs. The investigator heard one orchestra of eleven pieces in Doolittle School (85 per cent), which played remarkably well. All but one of the children were Negroes. A teacher in Webster School (30 per cent), where there was reported to be constant friction between Negro and white children, gave an incident of a Negro boy in the school playing the violin with a white accompanist and being enthusiastically applauded by the children.

The principal of a 92 per cent Negro school (Colman) reported an unpleasant experience when pupils from her school were invited to take part in a musical program at a West Side Park.

> A group of sixty went with two white teachers in charge. On the way over a group of foreign women called out insulting remarks to the teachers, but no one paid any attention. After the program the group started marching out of the park and were met at the gate with a shower of stones. The teacher told the children to run for their lives, and they all had to scatter and hide in the bushes in the park or run toward home if they could. A rough set of boys had got together and were waiting for those children, stones all ready to throw. Since that time we have never accepted an invitation to sing outside our own neighborhood. Invitations have come from time to time, but the children all come with excuses. All of them, children and parents throughout the neighborhood, are afraid but you can't get anyone to come out and say it. . . .

2. High Schools

CLASSROOM AND BUILDING CONTACTS

In the high schools the ordinary contacts in classes and about the building become subordinate to the more difficult problems created by the increased number of social activities—athletics, gymnasium exhibitions, clubs, and parties.

The dean of Englewood High School, which has only about 6 per cent Negro children, said that the white and Negro children mingled freely with no sign of trouble or prejudice but thought that if more Negro children came to the school the spirit would change. A teacher in this same school who had formerly been at Wendell Phillips, where the majority are Negro, said that a spirit of friendliness had grown up there between the two races, and race distinction had disappeared.

There was only one Negro teacher in the high schools of Chicago at the time of this investigation, the teacher of manual training at Wendell Phillips. He is a graduate of the University of Illinois and had substituted around Chicago for several years. Although they spoke very highly of him, none of the principals of three high schools with small Negro percentages and in which there were vacancies could use him. The principal of Wendell Phillips, with a large proportion of Negroes, told, however, of a different experience when this teacher was at that school. "In answer to complaints by pupils I told them that this man was a graduate of the University of Illinois, a high-school graduate in the city, and a cultured man. 'Go in there and forget the color, and see if you can get the subject matter.' In the majority of cases it worked."

Racial friction about the buildings and grounds was not reported by any of the high-school principals. "I have not known of a fight between a colored and a white boy in fifteen years," said the principal of Hyde Park.

Two principals said that the Negro children voluntarily grouped themselves at noon, either eating at tables by themselves in the lunch-room or bringing their own lunches and eating in the back part of the assembly hall. The gymnasium instructor at Wendell Phillips said that she had no difficulty in her work if she let the children arrange themselves. The gymnasium instructor at a school with a small proportion of Negroes said that the white girls had objected to going into the swimming-pool with Negro girls, but that she had gone in with the Negro girls, which had helped to remove the prejudice.

ATHLETIC TEAMS

In the field of athletics there seems to be no feeling between the white and Negro members of a school team, but the Negro members are sometimes roughly handled when the team plays other schools. "The basketball team is half and half," said the principal of Wendell Phillips. He reported some friction in previous years but said that "this year it is not shown at all." "They played a strenuous game with Englewood last week. A colored boy was roughly treated by the other team. Our white boys were ready to fight the whole Englewood team."

The principal of Hyde Park High School also said that there was no feeling in his school against Negro members of athletic teams, and that he did not know of a single instance in which a Negro boy was kept off an athletic team if he was the best for the place.

Two Seniors in a high school mainly white (Tilden) thus described the way they handled the Negro members of a visiting basket-ball team:

> On the way over here fellows on the outside bawled them out, but our fellows sure got them on the way home. There were three black fellows on the team and those three got just about laid out. Our team wouldn't play them, so there was a great old row. Then, when they went home some of our boys were waiting for them to come out of the building to give them a chase. The coons were afraid to come out, so policemen had to be called to take them to the car line. The white fellows weren't hurt any, but the coons got some bricks. . . .

SOCIAL ACTIVITIES IN HIGH SCHOOLS

In high schools, with their older pupils, there is an increased race consciousness, and in the purely social activities such as clubs and dances, which are part of high-school life, there is none of the general mingling often found in semi-social activities such as singing and literary societies. Although Negro pupils do not share in the purely social activities, they do not organize such activities among themselves.

"The colored never come to social affairs," said the dean of one school. "They are so much in the minority here that they leave all organizations to the whites." The principal of this school told of having seen two colored girls at a class party who danced together for a while and left. "It is the only time I've seen the two races at the same social gathering."

The dean of Englewood said: "We have colored children in singing clubs, in the orchestra, in literary societies, in class organizations, and on athletic teams. Always when there is a class party there will be five or six colored children. They will always dance together, but they are present and welcomed by the white. Between dances it is not uncommon to see white and colored talking."

An incident showing lack of feeling against individuals of special achievement was given by the principal of this last school:

> Several years ago we organized a voluntary orchestra which met after school. The director accepted all applications, among them a number of colored boys. The white boys balked; it should be white membership or they would leave. As it was near the end of the year the orchestra was dissolved. The next year I suggested to

the teacher that he fill the orchestra places by a general tryout, so understood, but really with the policy of excluding the colored. This was done and a white orchestra organized. Shortly, the father of H. F., a colored boy who had been excluded, protested in my office, saying that his boy had been excluded because of race prejudice and that he was going to carry his protest to the Board of Education, for he knew his boy played better than any boy in school. I admitted that it was a choice in the school of white orchestra or no orchestra, but that if his boy was the fine musician he said he was I would gladly see what could be done. Soon after that H. appeared on a school program and played with remarkable skill and technique. He was applauded enthusiastically and recalled three times. Straightway the orchestra members asked him to play with them. He became unusually popular throughout the school. His standing was the highest and he was awarded a scholarship of $100 allowed by the Board of Education for the best student. He was also chosen to represent the school on the Northwestern University scholarship, and in his Freshman year he won another scholarship for the next year. The death of his parents made it necessary for him to leave college to support his brothers and sisters. At this time he was stricken with infantile paralysis. The interest on Liberty bonds taken out by the high school is paid in to H., and when the colored people gave a benefit for him the pupils sold 500 tickets. He is improving and teaching violin to thirty pupils at present. His sister is in the school now on a scholarship and is doing remarkably well also.

At Wendell Phillips the situation was quite different, for there were no school or class social affairs which were general. There were invitational affairs to which the Negroes were not invited. All the clubs in the school were white, Negroes being excluded. The principal said he would not insist on mixed clubs until he saw the parents of the children mixing socially. The glee club was an especially difficult problem because of its semi-public as well as social character. The Negro children maintained that a glee club composed entirely of whites was not representative of a school in which the majority were Negroes. The Negroes had not responded to the suggestion of the principal that they form a glee club of their own, and as the white children would not be in a glee club with Negro children, there was constant friction over this club.

Other principals expressed the conviction that the racial problem of school social affairs could not be solved until the prejudice and antagonism of adults had disappeared. One principal said he had had to call off an arrangement for a class affair because the hotel would not accommodate the Negroes. Another principal thought that the schools would not wait to follow the lead of the parents in forgetting the race prejudice but would themselves be the greatest factor in destroying it.

6

EMORY S. BOGARDUS

The City Boy and His Problems: A Survey of Boy Life in Los Angeles

1926

In the late 1920s, concerned with the behavior of the city's youth, the Rotary Club of Los Angeles commissioned Emory S. Bogardus, a professor at the University of Southern California, to investigate "boy life" in the fast-growing metropolis, from the effects of automobiles and movies on the morals of youth to the absence of playgrounds and the formation of gangs. The City Boy and His Problems *contains verbatim testimony from hundreds of people. Bogardus identifies each person as, for example, "a boys' worker" or "a parent" at the end of each paragraph. The activities chronicled in Los Angeles resemble the behavior first described by child welfare activists more than a generation earlier, suggesting that city children and youth had not simply become unmanageable, but had begun to form a youth culture separate from that of their parents.*

The Automobile and Sex Problems

The "tough" boy who gets into repeated sex trouble usually tries to defend himself by saying that the girl leads him on by any one of a half a dozen wiles. She calls him a sissy if he does not meet her sex desires. They jump in an automobile and go off by themselves. There

Emory S. Bogardus, *The City Boy and His Problems: A Survey of Boy Life in Los Angeles* (Los Angeles: Rotary Club of Los Angeles, 1926), 74–75, 80–83.

is no supervision, of course. Most illicit sex relations occur in this way. (A boys' worker.)

The automobile is very potent in the life of the young people. I think it is the most important factor in what might be called downright immorality; a couple get off into the country in some secluded spot, and there are very few people who would not be tempted. I do not think we can blame the young folks too much. (A boys' worker.)

Then our autos; the couple go out for a ride, reach some secluded spot, and things go from bad to worse. Of course, that deals only with immorality. A fellow may steal and break all other laws, and be a perfect gentleman with a girl. But this perpetual spooning in all places leads to promiscuous relations. (A parent.)

The auto has been a very great contributing factor in creating the problem boy. When young people get out in autos they always want to go as fast as the car will go, and that gives an exhilarating effect upon the occupants and tends to break down the barriers that before existed. Then I think these skeleton cars are worse than the other type. Other things being equal, a couple in a sport car are more liable to step over the bounds than otherwise, simply because the car they are in is different, or a little off color, so to speak. (A boys' worker.)

After the party or the play, it is off to the beach, and then it is two or three before the couple are home again. I think the parents should be more careful, should know about when the party or play was to be over, and allow a reasonable time for Miss Mary to get home, and demand that she get there, and likewise Mr. John. Whenever auto rides are indulged in they ought to be awfully sure of the crowd that daughter or son are going with, and set a definite time, and insist that they are home by that time. (A parent.)

On his nineteenth birthday he was pinched for stealing a car off the street. He told the judge it was his birthday, and his father would not let him use their machine, and he had a date with a girl, so he thought he would borrow a car. That same night he and his gang went on a "wild ride" to the country. The girls they had were not girls from their town, but girls passing through the town in a musical show. L——— had his first illicit sex relations. From that time on, for the next six months, he became worse in his attitude toward his home. His father finally heard of his relations with women and girls, and turned him over to the courts. The boy resented this act of his father's very much. His mother became worse and refused to see the boy. The sisters would have nothing to do with their brother. (A boys' worker.)

The Cabaret and Public Dance Hall

As institutions, the cabaret and public dance hall have much to answer for in connection with the welfare of older boys. Some dance halls are especially bad, with their small dancing floors, atmosphere of smoke, punch that "nearly punches you out," and dancing which is mildly described as lascivious. High school boys, with their girl friends, are present on Friday and Saturday evenings. The appeal to the sex passions as told by boys who participate is beyond all decent description.

Some of the "road houses," outside the city limits, are also patronized by boys and girls. Conditions in these are often much worse than in the halls within the city. Many are under little or no supervision at times.

I had expected to find more young people of the high school and college age, but the Negro who ran the men's washroom volunteered that "Friday night is kid's night." (A research worker.)

The dancing was simply disgusting in its lasciviousness. I had visited some of the lowest dance halls and dives in Europe, but never saw a worse exhibition of putrid dancing than last Saturday night at the "X." (A research worker.)

The more sophisticated and blase youngsters of the high school age saunter in around 9:30 and 10:30. One could not help but remark the number of old men dancing with young women. (A boys' worker.)

"The best part" about these dance halls is you don't have to know anyone to get along. And you can come in when you want and go out when you want. And you can get acquainted with the ones you want to know, and you can leave the others alone and they let you alone. (A boys' worker.)

The orchestra was about the average one, producing good jazz that fairly makes a cripple want to dance, but they were more vocal than usual and sang several songs during the course of the evening. Amongst their selections were several verses of an improvised "It ain't a gonna rain no more," and some of these verses were simply filth. (A research worker.)

As long as boys are in the Valentino stage,[1] dance halls will remain a problem. We close our dances at 11:30, and then the young people go off to some public dance hall that is still open, so we have been keeping ours open longer. It's a big problem. (A boys' worker.)

[1] Rudolph Valentino (1895–1926), romantic silent movie star.

Although the whole atmosphere is rather more amusing and ridiculous than vicious and dangerous, still it is not a healthy atmosphere for high school students. They cannot help but imbibe some of the cynicism and hectic, artificial, selfish seeking after foolish pleasures of their elders. Most of the women present were smoking. (A research worker.)

Anyone who has seen it will agree, unless they are hopeless, that it is a veritable cesspool of filth and no fit place for anyone to spend much time, let alone high school students. I should strongly recommend that such places be compelled to pay a license high enough to permit of the city stationing a policewoman in each to supervise dancing and conduct generally, and that there be a stipulation in licensing that there be adequate floor space for dancing provided, so that there will be no temptation for closely packed humanity to let its hands stray. (A boys' worker.)

Cheap Magazines, Newspapers, and So Forth

The part that cheap magazines play in the lives of many boys and girls is large. They are read for their sexually suggestive jokes. At house parties of questionable moral character, so the police report, are found current copies of the worst. The dime novel of the past has been supplanted by the questionable short story and cheap magazine.

These newspapers which play up the diseases of society in lurid and exciting headlines are creating distorted views of society in young minds. The newspaper that depicts a robbery or murder, showing where the offender stood when he shot, is putting dangerous pictures into minds of youth. When burglary is made to look heroic, newspaper standards need revising. A leading newspaper in a middle western state has awakened to its guilt and has inaugurated a new policy of putting all pathological stories on the second page and of using ordinary headlines.

Penny arcades contain pictures that arouse the passions of youth. In order to get the nickels, these passions may be falsely stimulated. Immoral young women are reported as frequenting some of these places, and dope peddlers find in them convenient places to ply their trade.

Cheaper pool halls in the poorer downtown districts are "hangouts" for boys and young men. As centers for exchanging indecent stories and planning raids, they lower social standards.

"Side Shows" and "Dancing Girl Shows" cater to older boys' desires for thrills. The price is cheap and the appeal to passion is high.

CHEAP MAGAZINES

I think that we are making a big mistake in not suppressing all of these which these boys so freely condemn; these "kids" are not goody goodies, either. (A boys' worker.)

The magazine literature that the fellows read has a very large influence on them. Many of them read these kinds that do not have a very elevating effect on a fellow. The worst are imported from France. (A police officer.)

Four couples up in the mountains traced their misconduct to reading "smutty magazines." In one city they have recently legislated seventeen magazines off the news stands because of their demoralizing effect upon boys and girls. (A police worker.)

"Smutty magazines" are read extensively by the boys, and by girls too, for that matter. That is the kind of girls some boys go with. Many of them read these and throw them down on the living room tables at home and their parents don't say anything about it. Others smuggle them in and read them in private. (A parent.)

STUDIES OF CHILDREN AT WORK

Hundreds of thousands of children worked in textile mills in small southern towns, in coal mines in Appalachia and elsewhere, on farms and ranches throughout rural America, and on the streets and in the sweatshops of small and large cities alike. Although advocates for child labor regulation generally ignored agricultural labor, most of the other varieties of child labor were targeted by Progressive reformers. As they had for the issues of recreation and moral development, researchers sought to obtain basic facts about the extent of child labor, the kinds of work that children were doing, and its possible ill effects. The National Child Labor Committee and its various local and state branches commissioned studies of most states and many municipalities. NCLC researchers and writers investigated countless factories and sweatshops, calculated wages and hours for thousands of children and their families, and estimated the cost to child workers of sparse educational opportunities and poor health care.

7

E. N. CLOPPER

Children on the Streets of Cincinnati
1908

This study of child workers in Cincinnati street trades exemplifies child labor research and provides a good summary of the range of work done by children on most American city streets. E. N. Clopper was secretary for the Ohio Valley States, National Child Labor Committee. In one of the article's few touches of drama, Clopper describes an incident that proved a consistent charge made by reformers against street work: It taught boys to cheat, fight, and behave in many other inappropriate ways.

Newsboys

As in other cities, the great majority of children engaged in following the street trades in Cincinnati are newsboys. There are about 1,900 regular newsboys in the city, of whom approximately one-fifth are negroes. The Newsboys' Protective Association was organized for these boys in January, 1907, and club rooms were provided in the downtown district. The association is supported by subscription and by the proceeds from entertainments. Certain wealthy business men of the city have guaranteed its maintenance in case of financial embarrassment. A reading room, a gymnasium and baths have been installed and the services of a superintendent who gives all of his time to the club, have been secured. Here boys congregate in the evening and at other hours when not engaged in selling papers, the object being to get them off the street during their leisure hours. The attendance, however, is small. The present membership of the association is nearly 500, but the average daily attendance during February, March and April of this year was only 56, three-fifths of these being white and the rest colored. The attendance is greater during the school vacation period. The superintendent co-operates with the truant officers and the probation officers connected with the juvenile court, to the end that as many of the boys as possible shall attend school.

E. N. Clopper, *Child Labor and Social Progress: Proceedings of the Fourth Annual Meeting of the National Child Labor Committee* (Philadelphia: American Academy of Political and Social Science, 1908), 113–19, 123.

The morning newspapers are distributed almost entirely by youths and men, the boys, as a rule, handling only the afternoon papers. Except during the baseball season there is ordinarily no demand for these papers after seven o'clock in the evening, the last edition being issued at half-past two in the afternoon. Consequently the boys have their winter evenings free. But during the summer they are in the streets with the sporting editions usually until nine o'clock. The majority return home as soon as their papers have been sold, but many remain in the downtown district until late at night, some begging money from passersby, others offering chewing gum, shoe strings or lead pencils for sale, but in reality also begging, others lingering about the five-cent theatres and flitting around from place to place, generally absorbed in the evil features of the city's life. The number of girls who sell newspapers in the city is very small indeed, and officers spare no efforts to discourage and prevent the practice. In fact, the girls so employed are so few that they do not form a factor in the problem.

Children as young as five years of age sell papers in the residence districts. The branch offices of the afternoon newspapers sell to the newsboys at the rate of two copies for one cent, the children earning half a cent by the sale of every copy. Little five-year-old tots begin their careers by purchasing two copies and earn a cent by their sale each afternoon. Some of the older boys dispose of as many as three hundred copies daily, thus earning $1.50 in two or three hours, but thirty-five or forty cents represents the average amount earned in one day. Newsboys may return all unsold copies and be reimbursed at the purchase price, but this is done only in rare instances, for the children persist until all their copies have been sold.

The situation in Cincinnati is greatly aggravated by the policy pursued by agents of two afternoon newspapers to maintain and extend their circulation. A number of bullies are employed whose principal duty is to follow the newsboys who sell the opposition paper and threaten and harass them if they are found trying to sell more than a specified number of copies. One paper allows the newsboys to purchase ten copies of the opposition sheet, and if any boy is found with more than this number for sale, a bully swoops down upon him, sometimes strikes him if the time and place are favorable, and the privilege of selling more editions of that paper is taken away. One afternoon recently the writer stood on one of the busiest corners in the downtown district and watched this warfare. Several boys were there, selling the final edition of one of the two rival newspapers. Suddenly a small band of young men, all negroes, appeared with copies of the other paper and instead of entering into fair competition with the boys, deliberately got in front of them and harassed them wherever they went, to prevent their making sales. They even drove away a crippled boy who had been hobbling around on crutches, trying to sell a few copies. They did not dare strike the boys, as the place was too public, but they succeeded in curtailing their sales. The circulation manager of one of these newspapers, when questioned regarding the matter, admitted that he had in his employ five bullies, but claimed he had been obliged to resort to such methods in self-defense, as the other paper had instituted the practice and employed a larger number. The circulation manager of the other paper, when asked about the matter, declared that those were conditions that obtained years ago and that nothing of the kind was done to-day. The effect of such treatment upon the developing minds of boys can well be imagined, and it is to be hoped that these newspapers will soon adopt a policy fairer to the boys and worthier of the journalistic profession.

Formerly every newsboy had a badge bearing a number, and his name and address were recorded in the newspaper office so that assistance could be rendered if necessary when a boy fell ill or met with accident or other misfortune, but the badges have been lost and the effort abandoned. The following statistics, covering four hundred newsboys, it is believed fairly indicate the conditions surrounding the entire body of these little business men in Cincinnati:

NATIONALITY		AGE	NO.	DOMESTIC CONDITION	
American, white	123	7	3	Both parents living	
colored	116	8	10	(including step-parents)	302
German	86	9	21	Father dead	59
Jewish	36	10	36	Mother dead	22
Irish	25	11	49	Both parents dead	16
Italian	5	12	79	Married	1
English	3	13	63		—
Dutch	3	14	52	TOTAL	400
Hungarian	2	15	26		
Indian	1	16	21	EDUCATION	
	—	17	16		
TOTAL	400	18	9	Attending school	322
		19	6	Not attending	78
		20	4		—
		Over 20	5	TOTAL	400
			—		
		TOTAL	400		

The minimum age limit at which a child may be employed legally in any gainful occupation in Ohio is fourteen, and in this connection it is interesting to note that of the four hundred newsboys, two hundred and sixty-one are under fourteen, and that the age at which the maximum number of boys engage in selling newspapers is twelve. This holds for both white and colored boys. Of the white newsboys, twelve per cent are not in school, but twelve of the number are over sixteen years of age, leaving only eight per cent of the entire number of white boys who are under sixteen and not in school. Of the colored boys, thirty-eight per cent are not in school, but twenty-eight of the number are over sixteen years of age, leaving fourteen per cent of the entire number of colored boys who are under sixteen and not attending school.

The number of orphans and half orphans among these children is far less than is generally supposed. But the presence of both parents in the home is not always a guarantee of happiness to the child. One little fellow said his brother and sister didn't stay at home, and he didn't know where they were. Another said his parents lived elsewhere, and that he had been left with relatives. In another case the parents had been separated and the children were living with their mother in two rooms. One boy said his father had left home when he was a baby, and that he sold papers and helped at home. Another boy's father had run away six years ago and had never been heard from since. The father of one was in an asylum for the insane. In another case the boy's father had left home, the mother had married again and now conducts a saloon, the bartender being her second husband. One case was found where a family of five persons occupied two rooms; another where ten lived in four rooms; and another where seven were cooped up in three.

There are about ten thousand Italians in the city, the majority being Sicilians, and the average number of children in a family is four. The experience of workers among these people has shown that the Italians are much more careful of the welfare of their children, and especially of their daughters, than is generally supposed. They do not allow their girls to go to work anywhere unless two go together, and if there be no suitable companion the child must remain at home. Nearly half a century has elapsed since the city hospital was built, but in all that period, the records, it is said, show not a single Italian girl ever admitted into the ward where disreputable characters are treated. The Italians seldom if ever desert their children, but they have not yet learned that the school is a better training ground than the street.

Fruit Vending

Almost all the Italian children who work are engaged in fruit vending or basket selling. In a canvass of 77 Italian children, the distribution among various occupations was as follows:

Fruit venders	44	Bootblack	1
Basket sellers	13	Organ grinder	1
Newsboys	8	In shooting gallery	1
Delivery boys	3		
Odd jobs	2	**TOTAL**	77
Errand boys and girls	4		

Of this number, 55 were Sicilians, 15 Neapolitans, 5 Genoese, 1 Lombard and 1 Calabrese.

Of the 44 fruit venders, 24 were boys and 20 were girls; 41 were attending school and three were not; one was an orphan; the average age was thirteen; the average daily amount of sales, $1.42; the average number of hours devoted daily to this work five, part of the time being before school but most of it after dismissal, the hours ranging from a minimum of three to a maximum of seven daily. The three children who were not attending school were aged respectively twelve, thirteen and fourteen years; the twelve-year-old boy was found to be working ten hours daily, in charge of a fruit stand in front of his father's store, his mother is demented, his father is old, the boy is the eldest child in the family and gives all his earnings to his parents. The thirteen-year-old boy was working with his father, pushing a fruit cart from eight to ten hours a day, but, as with practically all Italian children, he was not allowed to handle any money. The fourteen-year-old boy was found pushing a cart and tending a stand in market, working twelve hours a day, his sales amounting to $3.25 on an average; this boy maintains a family of five persons, his younger sister is blind and his father is dead.

The ages of these little fruit venders are as follows: Seven years, 1; 9 years, 2; 10 years, 3; 11 years, 1; 12 years, 14; 13 years, 20; 14 years, 3. Total, 44.

The majority of Italian children engaged in this line of work tend stands in front of their parents' stores, and when anyone stops to make a purchase, the father or mother is called to take the money. One ten-year-old boy works six hours daily in the market, part of the time before and part after school, there are six children in the family and one is a deaf mute. A thirteen-year-old boy works four hours out of school daily and eighteen hours on Saturday, tending a stand in front of his father's store and driving a fruit wagon. Another boy of the same age works seven hours daily besides attending school, and on Saturday he rises at five in the morning and retires at a half hour before midnight, his sales on this day amounting to three dollars. A little girl of eleven years tends a fruit stand five hours daily and also goes to school; she has two brothers over fifteen years of age who cannot read.

Other Trades

Of the thirteen basket sellers, nine were girls and four were boys. Their ages range from nine to thirteen years. All were Sicilians, there were no orphans among them, and all were attending school. Their average age is eleven, average daily amount of sales eighty-five cents, and average number of hours devoted daily to the work four, part of the time before and part after school. On Saturdays these children work in the market from fifteen to eighteen hours, their sales then amounting to about three dollars.

The errand boys and girls earn on an average thirty-four cents per day during average time of three hours. Two do not attend school; one of these is a little Lombard girl of thirteen years whose parents are separated. The other is a Sicilian boy of fourteen years who is small for his age, has just withdrawn from school and works six hours daily, his father is insane and has five children. This little fellow is the eldest child, and is soon to take a position in a tailor's shop as an apprentice at a salary of $4.50 per week. The one organ grinder found is thirteen years old and works two hours before school and again after school and all day Saturday, usually collecting from $2.50 to $3.00 on the holiday. The attendant in a shooting gallery is a Genoese boy of twelve years who works four hours daily besides attending school, and on Saturday and Sunday gives all his time to helping at this business, taking in as much money as his father does.

A little boy eleven years old was found who earned about three dollars a week working at anything he could find; there are five children in the family, the father is dead and the mother cannot speak English; this little boy attends school and works five hours daily. . . .

The law in Ohio provides that no child under fourteen years of age shall be employed in any gainful occupation; that children between fourteen and sixteen years of age, before securing employment, shall obtain from school superintendents certificates to the effect that they have successfully completed seven specified studies of the primary course, after having presented documentary evidence of age, or if unable to read and write English they may not be employed unless they attend day or night school during employment; and that no boy under sixteen or girl under eighteen shall be employed in any gainful occupation more than eight hours a day before six o'clock in the morning or after seven o'clock in the evening. The eight-hour provision will take effect July 1, 1908.

All this is good, but it is not enough. Some method must be found to apply this law practicably to the street trades of the large cities. Complete protection must be afforded every child under fourteen years of age. Even so, we cannot grant that society has fulfilled its entire obligation. Children fourteen and fifteen years of age are too young and undeveloped to take up such burdens of life, and may the day soon come when the minimum age limit for employment in gainful occupations shall be raised from fourteen to sixteen and the state make all necessary provision for the care of the few children who would otherwise be forced into premature toil because of their unfortunate circumstances.

8

UNITED STATES CHILDREN'S BUREAU

Industrial Home Work of Children
1922

As the only government agency with a direct interest in the youngest Americans, the United States Children's Bureau also studied child labor. This excerpt from a 1922 bureau study shows the extent and effects on children of the "home work" conducted in crowded urban tenements all over the United States. Unlike street work, which was dominated by boys, "home work" often involved girls—some as young as three years old.

Of the 2,338 children who had worked more than 30 days and had received compensation, 22 per cent stated that they began home work for the direct purpose of adding to the family income. In addition, nearly one-third reported that they began work to help other members of the family. Imitation of friends and neighbors and desire to earn spending money or money for war funds were other motives. Some parents used home work to keep their children busy and out of mischief.

More than half the scheduled children had stopped home work before the end of 1918, because of poor pay, interference with school work, or tediousness of the work, or for other reasons. A whole family usually stopped home work at the same time, just as it began and worked as a unit. The character of home work as a family occupation rather than as one in which individuals worked independently is shown by the fact that in more than 75 per cent of the families studied, persons over 16 years of age, usually the fathers and mothers as well as the children, were engaged in the work.

The children worked on about 100 varieties of factory work, distributed by 21 industries. The principal home occupations of children, in the order of their importance, were carding snaps (dress fasteners),

United States Children's Bureau, *Industrial Home Work of Children* (Washington, D.C.: U.S. Government Printing Office, 1922), 48–49.

stringing tags, drawing threads on lace, linking and wiring beads, setting stones, working on military buttons, carding shoe buttons, finishing underwear, carding jewelry, and putting together chain fasteners. This work consisted of very simple processes constantly repeated. Ninety-one children, however, worked on machines.

The family kitchen was the children's workroom in more than four-fifths of the houses visited. In many cases the lighting was very poor. More than four-fifths—1,963—of the children worked in the evening after supper, and 1,860 of these also worked at some other period during the day.

Eyestrain from home work was reported by 117 children. Many other children complained of sores, callouses, and blisters caused by their work. Some of the teachers reported that child home workers came to school tired and listless. In occupations where presses were used, accidents, chiefly the bruising or cutting of fingers, were frequent.

Almost half the 956 children who reported the maximum amount which they could earn in an hour stated that, working at top speed, they could not earn as much as 5 cents, while 45 reported an earning capacity of less than 1 cent an hour. More than one-fourth, 29 per cent, could earn from 5 to 10 cents an hour; 9 per cent could earn from 10 to 15 cents; 9 per cent could earn 15 to 25 cents; and only 3 per cent could earn 25 cents or more.

Family groups were the customary working units, and hourly earnings were obtained for 136 of these groups. The average earnings per group were a little over 11 cents an hour, and the average earnings per person, for the 469 home workers in the 136 groups, were a little over 3 cents an hour.

Of the 928 families reporting total yearly earnings from home work, only 4 per cent earned more than $200; 89 percent earned less than $100; and nearly three-fifths less than $25. The average annual earnings of these families were $48.17.[1]

It was reported that the standards set up by the State of Rhode Island for school children and children working in factories were violated by home-working children in the following cases:

Children of school age remained at home for extended periods or for a day now and then to do home work, contrary to the compulsory education law of Rhode Island; children under 14 did factory work at home, though the law prohibited them from working in factories;

---

[1] A typical factory worker in the 1920s made about $1,200 a year.

women and minors under 16 employed in factories did overtime work at home contrary to the spirit of the law limiting hours of work; and children injured in the course of home work were deprived of compensation under the workmen's compensation law.

School officials, social workers, and persons other than manufacturers who were interviewed in regard to industrial home work of children, had little information on the subject and attached small importance to it. The public schools countenanced home work to the extent of permitting children to do it in school as manual training work or to earn money for various "drives."

It was found that almost three-tenths of the home-working children between 9 and 13 years of age who reported their school grades were retarded, one-tenth of them being 2 or more years below what is commonly accepted as the standard for their ages. Retardation was more noticeable among the older children, as the percentages increased steadily with each year of age, from 15.6 per cent at 9 years to 43 per cent at 13 years.

A possible danger to the health of the community was found in the fact that large numbers of families reported the performance of home work while members of the family were ill with infectious diseases. In some cases the sick persons took part in the work. . . .

Testimony concerning Physical Injuries from Home Work

Many complaints were made by workers concerning the injurious physical effects of home work. Eyestrain was reported for 117 children during the year covered by the inquiry, and in numerous instances the workers stated that they had to begin wearing glasses as a result of carding snaps, linking and wiring rosary beads, stringing tags, and setting stones. One mother said that after her little girl had painted flags for 10 or 15 minutes she would complain that they "began to walk." Carding snaps made sores and blisters on fingers, and the pliers used in linking beads also caused blisters and callouses. Inexperienced workers at thread drawing on lace often cut their fingers on the threads.

Some of the teachers who were interviewed had observed signs of fatigue in certain children which they attributed to home work. An ex-principal said that home workers came to school in the morning tired and listless. He said he had also observed a lack of proper physical development which he traced to the performance of home work after school and late at night. Another teacher said she knew of cases where children were allowed no playtime at all and worked until late at night, and that these children came to school utterly exhausted. Another teacher reported that children came to school worn out because the whole family got up at 5 o'clock in the morning to do home work after working late the night before. . . .

ILLUSTRATIVE EXAMPLES OF FAMILY EARNINGS

Illustrative examples of family earnings during the year are given in this section. It must be borne in mind that many of the children worked in snatches rather than steadily, but the time devoted to the work and therefore lost for purposes of recreation or rest, as set over against the returns received, is important.

Two children did stone setting, for which they were paid from 4 to 8 cents per gross of stones. They worked after school, during the vacation period, and about three evenings a week, for a period of 12 months. The maximum amount earned during one week was 75 cents, and during the year they earned $14.

Two other children wired and capped rosary beads for 11 months and carded shoe buttons for 1 month. They worked after school and during vacation, and in the evening until 9.30 and sometimes, when there were rush orders, until 11.30. Their maximum weekly earnings were $1, and their total earnings for the year were $10, an average of less than 10 cents a week apiece.

A mother and two children, one of whom was engaged in regular employment all day, worked at thread drawing on lace. One of the children worked before school and during most of the day when there was no school, and the mother and sister helped her in the evenings. The earnings for the nine months during which the work was constantly in the house were $18.

Four workers, two children and their parents, assembled rosaries at 45 cents a dozen for 12 months. The children worked after school and during vacation. In the evenings after supper they were assisted by their parents until 9 o'clock. Their earnings for the year were $117, less than $2.50 per month per person. The mother said: "Rosary beads are interesting. I figure like this: I have two children and would rather be at home to get them something to eat at meal time. Only trouble with that work is that you have to stay right with it all the time or you won't make anything."

Five home workers carded snaps and worked on military buttons during a period of five months, with total earnings of $11. The home work was done not only after school, but in the evenings for three of the five months. Three school children and three adults who worked in a jewelry establishment during the day, worked in the evenings for two and a half hours for six months putting together chain fasteners and setting stones. Their total earnings for the six months were $22.79. Another family of seven workers wired rosary beads at 16 cents per 1,200 and carded snaps at one-half to three-fourths cent per gross. They worked during seven months and earned $115.

One family of five, frequently assisted by an aunt and a cousin, earned $621 in 1918, working the entire year. During six months the father had no other employment but home work. Six kinds of work were done—carding shoe buttons, carding snaps, putting together chain fasteners, linking cuff buttons, assembling military buttons, and setting stones. At one time two presses were in the house, which were used in the work on military buttons. . . .

Home Work as a Means of Supplementing Family Income

. . . In a number of these cases the father was dead or had deserted the family. One widow did home work for an entire year, being assisted in the evenings by her two daughters. The mother said she frequently sat up almost all night at the work, and that it "nearly put her eyes out." The earnings of this family from home work during the year were $182. Another widow worked on rosary beads and stone setting for two months and was assisted by her four children. She said they worked every night until 10. In the two months they earned $44.44.

Three little girls started thread drawing on lace because "father was ill and couldn't work much, and all the children had to help support the family." The girls worked after school and were assisted by their parents in the evenings. The mother stated that for several weeks she and the father worked all night two or three times a week. During eight months the total earnings of the family from this work on lace were $69. Three other children started home work because the family "didn't have enough money with only one man working." They carded shoe buttons and military buttons and wired rosary beads. The work was in the house for 10 months, and the total earnings were $15.

Another family worked at pairing, labeling, and packing shoe laces. The father was not well enough to go out and he and the mother and two sons, 13 and 14 years of age, spent 8 hours a day at the work for 7 months. Two other children assisted in the evenings. During the

11 months in which the work was in the house the earnings of the family were $789. These relatively high earnings were possible only through the full-time work of the father and two sons of school age.

"WE ARE DEVOURING THE BOYS AND GIRLS": THE CAMPAIGN AGAINST CHILD LABOR

Not all child welfare advocates relied on statistics and dry academic prose to make their case on behalf of children and youth. Like Jacob Riis and other muckrakers—journalists who exposed political and corporate corruption—some of them showed their outrage and passion. The poem, short story, and photographs that follow are typical of Progressive efforts to mobilize support by appealing to Americans' emotions.

9

ERNEST H. CROSBY

The Machines

1902

Ernest Howard Crosby (1856–1907) was a lawyer and state legislator from New York who became a social reformer. Although he generally supported the political system, Crosby was decidedly more radical than most politicians. He was a pacifist and an anti-imperialist (he opposed American expansion in the Caribbean and the Philippines following the war with Spain in 1898)—and, as his poem shows, he was a harsh critic of American industrial practices.

Ernest H. Crosby, *Swords and Ploughshares* (New York: Funk & Wagnalls Co., 1902), 79–82.

I

Br-r-r-r-r-r-r!

What are the machines saying, a hundred of them in one long room?

They must be talking to themselves, for I see no one else for them to talk to.

But yes, there is a boy's red head bending over one of them, and beyond I see a pale face fringed with brown curly locks.

There are only five boys in all on this floor, half hidden by the clattering machines, for one bright lad can manage twenty-five of them.

Each machine makes one cheap, stout sock in five minutes, without seam, complete from toe to ankle, cutting the thread at the end and beginning another of its own accord.

The boys have nothing to do but to clean and burnish and oil the steel rods and replace the spools of yarn.

But how rapidly and nervously they do it—the slower hands straining to accomplish as much as the fastest!

Working at high tension for ten hours a day in the close, greasy air and endless whirr—

Boys who ought to be out playing ball in the fields or taking a swim in the river this fine summer afternoon.

And in these good times the machines go all night, and other shifts of boys are kept from their beds to watch them.

The young girls in the mending and finishing rooms down-stairs are not so strong as the boys.

They have an unaccountable way of fainting and collapsing in the noise and smell, and then they are of no use for the rest of the day.

The kind stockholders have had to provide a room for collapsed girls and to employ a doctor, who finds it expedient not to understand this strange new disease.

Perhaps their children will be more stalwart in the next generation.

Yet this factory is one of the triumphs of our civilization.

With only twenty boys at a time at the machines in all the rooms it produces five thousand dozen pair of socks in twenty-four hours for the toilers of the land.

It would take an army of fifty thousand hand-knitters to do what these small boys perform.

II

Br-r-r-r-r-r-r!

What are the machines saying?

They are saying, "We are hungry.

We have eaten up the men and women (there is no longer a market for men and women, they come too high) —

We have eaten up the men and women, and now we are devouring the boys and girls.

How good they taste as we suck the blood from their rounded cheeks and forms, and cast them aside sallow and thin and care-worn, and then call for more!

Br-r-r-r-r-r-r! how good they taste; but they give us so few boys and girls to eat nowadays, altho there are so many outside begging to come in —

Only one boy to twenty of us, and we are nearly famished!

We eat those they give us and those outside will starve, and soon we shall be left almost alone in the world with the stockholders.

Br-r-r-r-r-r-r! what shall we do then for our food?" the machines chatter on.

"When we are piling up millions of socks a day for the toilers and there are no toilers left to buy them and wear them,

Then perhaps we shall have to turn upon the kind stockholders and feast on them (how fat and tender and toothsome they will be!) until at last we alone remain, clattering and chattering in a desolate land," growled the machines,

While the boys went on anxiously, hurriedly rubbing and polishing, and the girls down-stairs went on collapsing.

"Br-r-r-r-r-r-r!" growled the machines.

III

The devil has somehow got into the machines. They came like the good gnomes and fairies of old, to be our willing slaves and make our lives easy.

Now that, by their help, one man can do the work of a score, why have we not plenty for all, with only enough work to keep us happy?

Who could have foreseen all the ills of our factory workers and of those who are displaced and cast aside by factory work?

The good wood and iron elves came to bless us all, but some of us have succeeded in bewitching them to our own ends and turning them against the rest of mankind.

We must break the sinister charm and win over the docile, tireless machines until they refuse to shut out a single human being from their benefits.

We must cast the devil out of the machines.

10

CHILD LABOR BULLETIN

The Story of My Cotton Dress

August 1913

The Child Labor Bulletin, *sponsored by the National Child Labor Committee, usually published studious articles about child laborers and child labor legislation. But "The Story of My Cotton Dress" was written for middle-class children to make them aware of the less fortunate boys and girls who played such a large role in the nation's economy. It tells the "history" of a little girl's cotton dress, and of all the children who worked to make it, from cotton pickers to mill workers. The article was one of a series of child labor–related articles written for children; another was "Mr. Coal's Story," about boys working in coal mines.*

I have had another accident! A big tear in my pretty new dress. This time *I* want to mend it. When we went to Atlanta, Georgia, a few weeks ago, and saw the beautiful white cotton fields, mother told me how little boys and girls must help make most of the stuff used for our dresses. I used to think all other children had good times, and that going to school was very hard. Now I know better.

I appreciate my dresses more since I know that from the very beginning when the cotton is ripe in the hot sun, little boys and girls must pick it for my dresses, while their backs grow tired and their heads ache.

Mother also took me to a cotton mill, on that trip. I saw how the cotton bolls are brought to the mill and the fluffy soft white mass is combed and then spun from one bobbin to another, until it is the finest thread, like the ravelings from the tear in my new dress.

The bobbins whirl around on large frames in the spinning room.

Little girl "spinners" walk up and down the long aisles, between the frames, watching the bobbins closely. When a thread breaks, the spinner must quickly tie the two ends together. Some people think that only children can do this quickly enough, but that is not so, for in a great many mills only grown-ups work.

Child Labor Bulletin, 2 (Aug. 1913): 57–73.

Mary is one of the spinners. She was very sad. Standing all day long, she said, had broken down the arch of her foot and made her flatfooted, which is very painful.

Some people say it is good for the girls and boys to work—that all children should be industrious. But they do not stop to think that there is a right and a wrong kind of work for little girls and boys. Spinning for a little while a day *could be made* the right kind, but work in a spinning room from 7 o'clock in the morning until 6 o'clock at night *is* the wrong kind. It keeps the children out of school, it gives them no chance to play, and they cannot grow strong. Many spinning rooms have their windows closed all day, because the rooms must be kept damp or the threads will break. Now, like growing plants, growing girls and boys need fresh air as well as light and sunshine. But there are more than a million children in this country who do not have fresh air, or play, or school because they are working. And of these there are enough in the cotton mills to make a big cityful.

When a bobbin is filled, the "doffer boy" comes along, takes it off the spinning frame and puts an empty bobbin in its place.

Many doffer boys and girl spinners grow up without learning to read or write, and without even hearing of George Washington.

Sometimes the machine is so high and the boys are so little, they have to climb up to reach the bobbins. If they slip they can hurt themselves badly.

At last the thread is ready to be woven into cloth. It is put through a machine called the warper, which prepares the threads which run the length of the goods. I think the hardest work the girls in the mill did was to thread every one of these warp threads through a tiny hole to prepare them for the loom that weaves the cloth.

"Surely, mother," I said when we left the cotton mill, "little girls can't do any more work for a dress."

"Ah, yes, dear," she said, "it is in the making of the dress itself that little girls take a big part. The cloth you saw woven is sent to factories in other large cities. It is cut into dresses that are carried in bundles into tenement homes. And such homes! Often only one or two rooms for the whole family to cook and eat and sleep and sew in. Mothers sew the dresses, while their little girls help draw out the basting threads and sew on the buttons.

"Not long ago I read the story about Rose, nine years old, who sews buttons on little girls' dresses. Her mother used to make dolls' dresses, and Rose had to snip them apart. She grew so tired of doing this for dolls for other little girls to play with, when she had no doll herself and when she wanted to read fairy stories, that what do you think she did? She snipped into the dolls' dresses with the scissors! So now her mother makes big dresses, for little girls, and Rose cannot use the scissors, but must work with a needle. She sews on 36 buttons to earn 4 cents."

"The scallops of the embroidery trimming little girls like so well for their dresses," mother continued, "are cut out by children in tenement houses. These little girls generally go to school, but often fall asleep over their lessons because they worked long after bedtime the night before, and an hour or two before school in the morning.

"The pretty ribbon trimmings are pulled through the dresses by children in still other tenement homes. You see, their mothers do not mean to be cruel, but they must pay rent and buy coal and bread and shoes with the money the children can earn. More cruel than these poor mothers were the people who, when the fathers were little boys, made them do work that taught them nothing; for now the fathers do not know how to earn enough money, and they are idle while the children work.

"If only everybody cared, and would not buy things that children make, the factory men would give the work to the fathers and not to the children."

11

LEWIS HINE AND THE NATIONAL
CHILD LABOR COMMITTEE

Images of Children at Work

1908–1921

Lewis Hine (1874–1940) is best known for documenting the many varieties of child labor in the United States early in the twentieth century. A native of Wisconsin, Hine had worked in a furniture factory as a teenager and as a teacher in New York City. From 1908 to 1921, however,

Library of Congress, Prints & Photographs Division, National Child Labor Committee Collection, Reproduction Numbers LC-USZ62-107335, LC-USZ62-29093, LC-USZ6-632, LC-USZ62-121885, and LC-USZ62-99382.

he was the staff photographer for the National Child Labor Committee, shooting thousands of photographs during his travels throughout America. Published in NCLC pamphlets and books, displayed in exhibits, and used to illustrate lectures on child labor, his photographs captured working children of all ages on the job and during leisure moments. Hine's handwritten captions chronicled the names and ages of many of the children, and he occasionally remarked on their tiny stature, lack of education, or pitiful wages. Some of the children he photographed appear lost among the machinery that dwarfs them or on the busy streets where they work; others project an understandable weariness. Still others reveal a cockiness often noticed—disapprovingly—by child welfare reformers.

Opposite: Little girl working as a spinner in Mollahan Cotton Mills, Newberry, South Carolina.

John Tidwell, a young worker in a cotton mill, smoking a cigarette, Birmingham, Alabama.

Newsboy in St. Louis.

Flashlight photograph of messengers playing poker in the "Den of the Terrible Nine" (the waiting room for Western Union messengers, Hartford, Connecticut).

Home workers making artificial flowers in tenement at 302 Mott Street, New York City.

2

A Right to Childhood

When Florence Kelley declared in 1905 that all humans had "a right to childhood," she set the tone for Progressive child welfare reformers, who made establishing and protecting that right their chief focus. But what did a right to childhood mean? That question was partially answered by the researchers and writers who chronicled the problems facing children. Finding solutions to those problems would provide the rest of the answer. The documents in this chapter suggest some of the creative and far-reaching approaches to children's issues that reflected these developing notions of the rights of children.

THE NURTURE AND PROTECTION OF CHILDREN

Progressives were fond of making lists of the ways in which the lives of children should be improved. One such list came in 1924, when the League of Nations—formed just five years earlier after the First World War—adopted the Declaration of the Rights of the Child. It included the rights

to develop materially and spiritually;
to be fed, nursed, disciplined, and sheltered;
to be the first to receive help in times of crisis;
to be educated to a trade, and be protected from economic exploitation;
to be taught generosity and compassion for fellow men and women.

Many of those notions of childhood had appeared in earlier lists articulated by American Progressives.

12

EDWARD T. DEVINE

The Right View of the Child

April 25, 1908

Like Florence Kelley, Edward T. Devine, editor of the reform magazine Charities and the Commons, *believed that children possessed certain rights. The rights he laid out in his 1908 editorial were identical to the goals of the child welfare reformers: better health for infants and children, opportunities for constructive play, educational practices that prepared students to support themselves and to be useful citizens, guarantees that the government and the legal system would treat all children fairly and compassionately, and assurances that youngsters would be able, through their own hard work and determination, to improve their economic circumstances. Devine's almost impossibly optimistic editorial provides a perfect introduction to the articles on specific programs that appear later in this chapter.*

In certain cotton-raising districts of the South there is a strange saying that cotton and ignorance go naturally together. A man's wealth—that is to say not his well-being, which would be right enough, but his money income—is measured by the number of his children, and not, as it should be, by the efficiency of the adult. Could there be a clearer expression of the old, discredited view of the child? The bag slung about the neck for the cotton is made to fit the child, while the school term is adjusted not to the child but to the working season. The child is the center of the economic world and not the center of the educational and domestic world, and this means that the child is for exploitation and profit, rather than for nurture and protection. Thus cotton and ignorance are linked together—not naturally, but most unnaturally, and the industry which is otherwise the pride of the South and of America is blighted, not only in the mill but from the hour of its planting, joining the sweated industries of the northern cities and the glass works of northern towns as an active cause of race degeneracy

Edward T. Devine, *Charities and the Commons,* 20 (Apr. 25, 1908): 123–25.

and race suicide. Though it may be reprehensible for the race to perish for lack of births, it is a more shameful thing to destroy the vitality, to dwarf the minds, to refuse the natural and necessary protection of childhood to the children who are born into the world.

The new view of the child, which we may place against this background, has not been revealed by any single miraculous illumination. Would that some apostle on the way to Damascus could have a glorious vision of the divinity indwelling in the soul and body of the unspoiled child! But it is not so that social workers are guided to the formulation of their new ideals.

Piecemeal and fragmentary is the process by which we put together the outlines of the society which we would create; doubtful and arduous the advance towards it. The new view of anything, if it is a true and useful view, is likely to be but a synthesis, or a new interpretation, of old ideas; a convincing statement which we may all comprehend of ideas long held here and there by a few people of extraordinary insight. It is not necessary, as Socrates thought, that philosophers become kings, or kings philosophers, but only that the speculations of the philosopher be put into language which kings may understand. We, therefore, we citizens and kings of America, not setting ourselves up as philosophers, in describing our new view of the child may justly appropriate some of the fragmentary older new views which have been gained from time to time.

We may begin by urging the right of the conceived child in the mother's womb to be born. When the Children's Bureau is established in Washington it may well begin its labors by an investigation of sterility, abortions and still births. The new view, the religious view, the social view, the physiological view, the rational view of the child from every standpoint is that the right to birth itself must not be abridged. If disease interferes with it, then disease must be overcome. If deliberate crime interferes with it, then crime must be punished. If unscrupulous medical skill interferes with it, that medical practice must be brought more completely under professional ban and criminal prosecution. If ignorance and vicious indulgence interfere with it, then education at an early age by parents and teachers and physicians and others must take the place of the conspiracy of silence. If the employment of women in factories interferes with it, then that employment must be curtailed.

The right to be well-born is followed, in the new view of the child, by the right to grow up. We are doing better than our forefathers in this respect. Two hundred years ago in London, three-quarters of all the children that were born died before the completion of their fifth year. Decade after decade that percentage has been pushed down until now it is something like twenty-five instead of seventy-five per cent.

Even now, in 1900, in the registration area of the United States, the death rate for all children in their first year is 165 in the thousand. Milk poisoning, ignorance of mothers as to how to feed and care for their children, inability to nurse them, either for physical or for economic reasons, lack of necessary facilities for surgical and medical treatment, and lack of knowledge in the rank and file of the medical profession concerning the diagnosis and treatment of infantile disorders, are among the causes for this high mortality among infants. The greatest advances of medical science have been in this field, and the substantial reduction in the death rate of many communities is due to the saving of the lives of babies more than to reduction at any later age. It is the new view, the social view, that this process should be carried farther, and that those who are born shall be permitted not only to survive, but to become physically healthy and strong. The Children's Bureau, which is to be for investigation and publicity, not for administration, will deal with that subject also. The Federal government should study continuously the problems of illegitimacy, infant mortality, illiteracy, feeble mindedness, orphanage, child dependence, and child labor, just as it studies, and properly studies, the soils, the forests, the fisheries and the crops.

The third element in the new view of the child is that he has a right to be happy, even in school. Pestalozzi and Froebel[1] helped us to think that out. Jane Addams has suggested that one day we shall be ashamed of our present arguments for the prohibition of child labor,—that it is physically destructive and educationally disastrous, although these seem like reasonably adequate arguments to start with, and shall recognize that the joyousness of childhood, the glorious fulness of enjoyment for which children are by nature adapted, and by their Creator intended, is in itself a worthy end of legislation and social concern. Bronson Alcott,[2] of whom it is said that his greatest contribution to American literature was his daughter, says that a happy childhood is the prelude to a ripe manhood. It is no artificial,

---

[1]Johann Pestalozzi (1746–1827) and Friedrich Froebel (1782–1852) promoted educating young children through play and informal activities. Froebel inspired the kindergarten movement in Europe and the United States.

[2]The educational reformer Bronson Alcott (1799–1888) used nature, art, and music in his child-centered classroom. His most famous student was his daughter, the writer Louisa May Alcott.

hothouse, forced development of something which might be called happiness that we seek, but the spontaneous activity and growth of a protected, unexploited childhood.

It is a part of this new view, fourth, that the child has a right to become a useful member of society. This implies industrial—or stating it more broadly—vocational education. It supports the suggestion made by Mr. Noyes in one of the publications of the National Child Labor Committee that the school day might well be made longer, with greater variety in curriculum; and that the work which we deny, and rightly deny, in the factory for profit, may be demanded in the school for an hour or two or more daily for education and training. The disingenuous arguments as to the educational value of specialized long continued factory labor may be tested by the willingness of those who make them to introduce genuinely educational employment with the element of profit eliminated, into the school curriculum, where alone it belongs. Industrial efficiency is diminished or destroyed and not increased by child labor.

There is one final element in the new view of the child, the right to inherit the past more and more fully, the right to begin farther and farther along, the right not only to begin where the parent began—even that is denied when through destroying the strength and retarding the education of children, race degeneracy sets in—the right which we now assert is the right not only to be protected against degeneracy, but the right to progress. It is the new view of the child, the American view, that the child is worthy of the parent's sacrifice, that he must mount upon our shoulders and climb higher, that not only in accumulated possessions, but also in mastery over the physical universe, in spiritual attainment, in the power to serve his fellow men and to glorify God, he shall rise above his father's level. It is not a new idea. Hector,[3] on the plains of Troy, had a notion that men might say of Astyanax that he was a far better man than his father, and perhaps they did, or would have done so had Hector lived to protect and rear him. In a given instance the plan may fail, but the plan itself is significant for the father and for the child. The American child is not unknown in text books and essays and fiction. He has been pictured as smart, precocious, disrespectful and offensive. The child of the rich and preoccupied American, and of the vain and indulgent American, has sharpened the pencil of the caricaturist. Kipling in Captains Courageous plucked such a child from the liner and put him at the work on

[3] Hector led the defense of Troy during the Trojan War, eventually dying in combat with Achilles. Astyanax, his infant son, was killed when the city fell.

a fishing dory on the Banks of Newfoundland which his regeneration required. The neglected and spoiled child of foolish indulgence, and the neglected and spoiled child of avaricious poverty, tend to develop similar or equally lamentable traits. In neither case is there recognition of these fundamental elements in what we have called the right view of the child—normal birth, physical protection, joyous infancy, useful education and an ever fuller inheritance of the accumulated riches of civilization.

CASE STUDIES OF PROGRESSIVE REFORM

Each of the documents in this section provides a case study of a Progressive reform campaign; each solution described is a direct response to a perceived problem. The first two articles come from the pages of *Charities and the Commons,* the leading reform journal of the early twentieth century. Published by the New York Charity Organization Society, the magazine regularly published detailed, optimistic accounts of reform efforts around the United States. The third article appeared in *The Crisis,* the monthly magazine of the NAACP, edited by W. E. B. Du Bois. Although *The Crisis* focused on civil rights and education issues, Du Bois devoted one issue each year to the subject of children—with scores of formal photographs of African American babies and children—and he occasionally included a piece on the institutions and programs identified with Progressivism.

13

LILIAN V. ROBINSON

The City of Hawthorne

November 4, 1905

"The City of Hawthorne," founded in a park in a poor neighborhood in Boston, combined two Progressive reforms: the creation of supervised recreational facilities that would entice children away from the busy, dangerous city streets on which they played, and a limited form of self-government

Lilian V. Robinson, *Charities and the Commons,* 15 (Nov. 4, 1905): 182–85.

designed to instill discipline and responsibility in even the smallest
children.

As in larger municipalities than the "city of Hawthorne," better health
has followed civic reform in the order of cause and effect, so with the
opening of the Hawthorne Club playground on the first of May, the first
six weeks of the work was given to the organizing of a scheme of self-
government, which carried with it a plan for delicate children.

Only the Hawthorne Club children—200 in number—were admitted to the playground, and these were not wholly unfamiliar with
attempts at self-government. The buying and selling of votes had been
tried and condemned in earlier committees organized by these children. The choosing of a mayor for the city of Hawthorne (the name
given the playground by the children) was by secret vote, and their
choice the best possible one. The mayor, however, though he now
scorned the buying and selling of votes, followed a local custom in his
first appointment. "My brother first, of course," he announced, when
appointing his police board—the other members electing the brother
(one of the most mischievous and irresponsible boys in the club) *as*
chief, in courtesy to the mayor who had appointed them.

For a week the children were left largely to themselves, and at its
end half were in a state of revolt, the other half terrorized. The "chief"
had "rigged up" a patrol wagon, and with a zeal never shown in any
other pursuit, made arrests after the fashion in vogue on a near-by
corner, where the carrying off of a "drunk," or the participants in a
street fight, is one of the sights of the district. The "chief" imitated the
speed of the patrol wagon, the "rushing in" of the unhappy prisoner
and going off at a breakneck run to the club cellar, where the luckless
child was "dumped." In his zeal for the cause he even arrested a boy
passing by (not a member of the club) "because he was a bad boy,"
not because of any particular offense. It is needless to say that such
children as ventured to go to the playground at the end of the week
were models of propriety. The "chief" meantime, had learned to love
his office and his pride in the good order of the "city" was so sincere
that another chance was given him to use his power more wisely.

Besides the mayor and police board, a street and park superintendent were chosen, aldermen, councilmen and a judge—the superintendent of the playground representing the governor of the state. The
following laws were made by the children themselves—the mayor, on

his own initiative, making a well-printed and cleverly decorated copy of them "for everyone to see":

I

No member of the city of Hawthorne shall meddle with or splash water from the fountain.

II

Not more than one member of the city of Hawthorne shall be allowed upon a swing at one time for more than five minutes.

III

No member of the city of Hawthorne shall enter the cellar without permission of the superintendent.

IV

No member of the city of Hawthorne shall injure the plants.

V

No member of the city of Hawthorne shall use bad language.

VI

No member of the city of Hawthorne shall throw rubbish in the playground.

VII

No member of the city of Hawthorne shall disobey the superintendent.

The punishments for offenses were planned by the children—dismissal from the playgrounds, for a longer or shorter time was first proposed by the majority. One child, a girl of eleven, then suggested that this would leave the offending children with only the noisy, dirty street to play in, "which wouldn't be good for their health," and her proposal for half an hour on a prisoner's bench "in the clean playground" finally won acceptance from all as "the best punishment."

At the end of six weeks the city of Hawthorne was well established; as a rule, excellent order was kept, and the children were enthusiastic over their self-government plans. But most of these children were ripe for self-government, as the club discipline was good before the self-government plan went into effect. It is doubtful whether a similar plan could succeed where good discipline did not exist, especially if the children were as young as ours—one hundred and fifty from five to ten; the other fifty under fourteen, with half a dozen exceptions. The most successful boards or committees were those of both boys and girls, not of boys alone or girls alone.

With the closing of school and the opening of the playground for all day, came the inauguration of the plan for delicate children. A trained nurse, who had had a successful hygiene class in the club for several years, took charge under a physician with a wide knowledge of children's diseases. A group of twenty children were chosen for the experiment; delicate children, or with tubercular tendencies, or mentally atypical—ten of the group from the Hawthorne Club, the other ten from St. Stephen's, Lincoln House and Hale House—all from the tenement district in which the playground is situated, and children not yet likely to reach the hospital dispensary or institution.

The plan was to keep the children in the playground through the day, giving them, first, the benefit of simple gymnastic exercises, outdoor games, etc.; second, simple lessons in hygiene; third, outdoor lunches in the early forenoon and afternoon. The lunches were an extension of the "pure candy counter" scheme . . . and to the chocolate which the children bought at cost were added milk and "educators"— a cup of milk and two educator crackers selling for a cent. Fruit was sometimes included, and eggs at a cent a piece, with the privilege of cooking them out of doors in miniature chafing dishes; also a soup made of wild mushrooms and milk, greatly prized by Italians and Jews.

The lunches were served and eaten in the playground on little tables, from an attractive ware, and a great point was made of the children first washing faces and hands at the playground fountain, where fresh water is continually supplied—each child using his own towel.

The plan of lunches was first put before the older members of the club—those who have belonged since its beginning, six years ago. It was then found that the children often came to the playground breakfastless, not necessarily because breakfast could not be obtained, but because they "were not hungry in the morning." At eleven appetite came, and the penny which each child had as a rule, the older children felt would be spent for the playground lunch instead of the cheap candy or pickle formerly bought. The lunches, as a matter of fact, succeeded well, growing more popular as the summer advanced—the older children often buying for the younger ones.

The "towel" question has been a somewhat difficult one, but the older children finally formed a class for towel making—the products of their work being turned over to the "towelless" children, and the fountain serving for the washing of towels by the children themselves.

A board of health of three children was formed after the second part of the playground scheme was well under way. These children, a girl of eleven and two boys of ten and eight, produced the following "rules for health"—the gleanings of their hygiene lessons. The rules are given verbatim—only the spelling is corrected. The children had but one or two slight suggestions in getting the rules in form:

BOARD OF HEALTH, CITY OF HAWTHORNE, RULES FOR HEALTH

If you are a consumptive don't spit on the floor or street. Destroy the spit.

Keep yourself neat and tidy and don't bum around.

Eat simple and nourishing food, such as plain meat, fruit, eggs, crackers, cream and cereals.

Wash your face, hands, ears, teeth and nails.

In summer take two baths a week, and a sponge bath every day.

When you get up in the morning take a few breathing exercises.

Take plenty of exercise.

Take plenty of regular sleep.

Don't eat between meals.

Don't eat cheap candy and pickles.

Don't let anyone use your own towel.

Keep clean houses.

Try and have sunny rooms. Dark and damp rooms are not healthy.

Children from five to ten should take special care of themselves.

Older children should help the little ones keep clean.

Keep fresh air in your house.

Dirt is bad.

Flies are bad.

Don't let garbage stand around.

Clean your closets steady.

Change your clothes every week promptly.

The street and park departments learned their part in the general scheme for health. The dirt area of the playgrounds, and the shrubs and vines which border it have been kept free from offensive matter, and are well watered with hose as often as dust rises—the watering doing much to cool and freshen the air on hot days.

Sickness plays such a grim part in the lives of tenement children that an enthusiasm for the pursuit of health is easily roused among them. Though the child may know nothing of suffering in his own person, the sickness of father or mother, of brother and sister comes very close to him. The child, when a girl (and often if a boy), knows that he must "clean the house" and sometimes cook because his mother is sick, and if his father is sick, food itself becomes a vanishing quantity. The problems which sickness brings into the homes are often confided to the club leader by a child of eight or younger, and an older sister of eleven or twelve will take great pride and interest in a plan for building up the health of the younger ones of the family.

So it seemed wise to interest the little mothers or the little fathers in our plan and to secure their co-operation as well as that of the parents. Indeed the older children prove our valuable allies, and the family groups with *esprit de corps* for the welfare of its youngest members comes to raise its entire standard of life. Careless for themselves, or willing to put aside for themselves as "foolish" nurse's or doctor's commands, an earnest co-operation may be given instead, when the welfare of the little one is concerned.

This is especially true of the Jewish people, with their strong family ties.

Each child's case is tabulated, and careful records will be kept for four years or more. Through the winter each group will be watched by its respective house, the groups coming together again next summer.

It is hoped that the children thus watched over and trained to hygienic ways of life may be saved from the hospital or institution which they would otherwise doubtless enter in later years.

A part of the summer plans included excursions to public baths, playgrounds and parks, and the children's attention was thus drawn to the larger city's efforts in behalf of her citizens' health and pleasure. A municipal orchestra, too, has been formed among the children, and "municipal concerts" have been given in the playground for the mothers. Babies belonging to the families of the "citizens," have had a standing invitation to the playgrounds and to "free rides" on the miniature buckboard which, under the direction of a policeman, has made constant rounds.

It is felt, of course, that a city playground and a congested tenement district are not ideal spots for health building schemes, but unfortunately, most of our children can have nothing better, and even a city playground and a tenement can be made reasonably hygienic, and an intelligent enthusiasm for the laws of health can do much for the city child.

14

WALTER E. KRUESI

The School of Outdoor Life
for Tuberculous Children

December 19, 1909

Although city children faced many daunting health problems early in the twentieth century, one of the most deadly—and most feared—was tuberculosis. The only effective treatment for the "white plague," as it was sometimes called, was fresh air and rest, both of which were in short supply in bustling, crowded, smoky cities. A number of cities established "outdoor" or "fresh air" schools to provide special classrooms for children with respiratory problems.

The School of Outdoor Life for Tuberculous Children at Parker Hill, Boston, has made such an impression of its value that it is being carried on through the winter jointly by the Boston Association for the Relief and Control of Tuberculosis which organized it, and the Boston School Board. The latter body is furnishing the teaching force, school room equipment, and an especially adapted building for storm shelter and headquarters. The association furnishes the teacher's assistant, housekeeping-teacher, cook, janitor, special equipment, food, and sees that the children are properly clothed. The home conditions are supervised jointly. The School Board has become so interested in the number and conditions of tuberculous children under its charge, that it has appointed a special committee to investigate these matters. It is expected that a sufficient appropriation will follow to pay for a general examination by specialists.

Through this outdoor school the children, instead of falling further behind their grades, will get a good education while the restoration of their health is in process. The school exercises and work of the day will continue to be developed on lines dictated by the physical needs of the children. The parts which are specified and formal will come

Walter E. Kruesi, *Charities and the Commons,* 21 (Dec. 19, 1909): 447–49.

before the free time in order that fatigue shall not limit the program, but only regulate the intensity of the free action. They will be carried on in the open air except during storms. The little desks and chairs will be on individual platforms of light construction. Blankets with pockets for the feet and legs will be provided when they are necessary. The children have been barefooted all summer and it is planned that they be provided with soft functioning shoes when protection from cold is necessary. The whole teaching method will really be that of Pestalozzi: to have all the training and education natural and based on physical experiences.

Taking tuberculous children, and those who are seriously threatened with tuberculosis, out of the ordinary school buildings, and the pressure of crowded classes, into the sunlight and open air for education, and the restoration and building up of their health, would seem to be a very reasonable project. In Germany, Switzerland, England, and other European countries, it has been practiced for ten years or more, until such provision is fast becoming general. In America, the first fresh air school was established last fall in Providence, R.I. An article describing this school was printed in *Charities and the Commons* of April, 18. It finished its year very successfully and its continuance was a matter of course. That school is conducted indoors, but with one side wall removed, so that there is certainty of constant fresh air. The normal school hours prevail, and there is as yet no special training, nourishment or adaptation of the curriculum.

The first real outdoor school in America, however, was that started on the top of Parker Hill, last July. This school was designed for the tuberculous children found by the examination of 1,250 of the younger members of families in which there was already known to be a case of tuberculosis. Some of them had already been sent for short periods to convalescent homes, for country week excursions and visits, and a few had had more or less treatment in hospitals for different troubles which really expressed the same fundamental condition.

It was called the School of Outdoor Life, and was intended to give a group of tuberculous children: First, fresh air; second, a sufficiency of the best food adapted for them; and third, a natural hygienic life. The school was equipped with a lean-to kitchen and pantry, two dressing rooms and closets, and a large shower bath. In connection there was a large tent used as a dining room and as a shelter during storms. The camp was located in an old orchard, the shade of whose trees furnished a pleasant resting place. Hammocks, reclining chairs, and large hay pillows made by the children themselves, together with blankets for use on colder days, and tents equipped with beds for emergencies completed the equipment.

The children came to the camp at eight o'clock in the morning, and at once prepared for breakfast, washing their hands and rinsing their mouths. Breakfast consisted of porridge, bread and butter, milk, and occasionally fresh fruit. After breakfast, and each of the other meals, the children went at once to brush their teeth and then to perform other duties. Regular crews were assigned to assist alternately in the different housekeeping operations, and these were trained carefully to do their work.

A garden plot was laid out, and a separate garden four feet by seven was assigned to two children who worked it together. In the center were three common gardens for flowers. The children planted, weeded, watered, and otherwise attended to these gardens with the greatest faithfulness, and with excellent results. By the middle of August they had tomatoes ripening, and good crops of lettuce and radishes. The progress of the buckwheat which was used as a frame or border for the whole garden, was an astonishment and delight to them. It is significant of their spirit that the common garden was always as well taken care of as their private ones, and that there were no depredations. In addition to the general gardens, the children planted beans and sunflowers along two buildings, and looked after them carefully, performing some delicate transplanting work successfully, when they discovered that even plants answer the laws of life requiring sunlight, elbow-room, a good circulation of fresh air and good nourishment.

In the middle of the morning an hour was devoted to quiet study of the plants, flowers, and other living forms about the children, and to the application of the observations as lessons in natural history.

Just before noon, an hour was given for free play. At first the pupils were too lifeless and weak to engage in any active sports, but within a week or two they developed into normal boys and girls. Finally, one of them timidly asked whether he would be allowed to climb into the trees. He said he had never been in a tree before, but that he would like to get a bigger view. Permission being given, all the trees were soon bearing happy burdens.

Dinner at the camp was a substantial meal partaken of with gusto and a general "can I have some more." The afternoon's duties and play were brought to a close by permission to go into the shower, after which followed a good supper and the homeward journey.

The physical results shown during the first eight weeks were satisfactory not only through a general gain of from two to ten pounds in weight, but through a remarkably increased spirit and cheerfulness. The children seem to take as much delight in one part of their personal hygiene as another, and their helpfulness to one another is delightful. At the end of fifteen weeks the examining physician declared that nine of the thirty-two who had been admitted during that period might be discharged as "arrested," and might return to their regular schools. These were all well-defined but incipient cases.

The cost of operating the camp has been borne entirely by voluntary subscriptions, and amounted during the first seven weeks to 25.7 cents a person each day for food, and 35.5 cents a person each day for administration and training. The food cost may be considered to be relatively high. This has been a matter of design, for special arrangements were made to get milk from a thorough-bred herd, and nearly one-half of the food expenditure has been directly upon milk and eggs. It is an interesting fact that but two of the children are of distinctly American parentage. Twelve are of Irish, eleven Jewish, four Turkish, six Polish, and one of Scotch parentage.

15

FELIX J. KOCH

Little Mothers of Tomorrow

October 1917

"Little Mothers" was a phrase often used to describe the young daughters of the working poor charged with caring for their younger siblings while both parents were at work. It also captures in a more positive light the participants in a Cincinnati program aimed at teaching girls proper child care techniques.

It was in a quiet nook of the big playground which surrounds the Douglass Public School on Walnut Hills—a suburb of Cincinnati—that we overheard them.

Felix J. Koch, *The Crisis* (Oct. 1917): 289–92.

"No," the teacher said, "we shouldn't make baby brother walk, if he doesn't want to. It'll hurt his legs—might even make him bow-legged for life!" Whereupon the little six-year-old, who had been helping keep eye on the infant, who sat on the edge of the wall before them (this being Saturday and the school yard a playground), waived the point before superior knowledge.

Come to think of it, it was wonderful—this work of teaching the little colored mothers of tomorrow what so many, many mothers of today do not know;—just what is best for the little babe;—just how to conserve the infant for the race! Instead of the little colored girls pouting and crying at being set to mind younger brothers and sisters, Dolly is delighted now when Mother gives her charge of the cunning little baby, and lets her put into practise the lessons in the schoolroom the day before.

Down in Cincinnati, where this unique form of endeavor is sweeping the schools by leaps and by bounds, they call it the Little Mothers' Movement. The girls who constitute a Little Mothers' class wear great shield pins, almost like a policeman's badge; and even as the boy scout uniform admits the boys through police lines on certain occasions, so the little mothers are admitted where there is illness, disaster—even as their own mothers are not!

"Tell us about the Little Mothers' League," we said to Dr. William H. Peters, the head of the Department of Health of the Queen City, and the prime mover in the work of organizing these leagues in the schools not long since.

"Our Department of Health," he replied eagerly, "is carrying on an active campaign to prevent infant mortality. It has eight infant milk stations, where doctors and nurses are in attendance, to show mothers how to keep their babies well. There are several other milk stations maintained by private societies. In Cincinnati, a list of all the stations, or the address of the one nearest to your home, will be sent you, if you will write or telephone to the Department of Health. At these stations pure milk for feeding babies can be bought at cost price. The Department of Health is thus doing its part toward saving the babies. But this is not quite enough!

"Over and above all we can do we need the help of every mother in the city, and, in turn, of all the girls—the care-takers, so often, of younger brothers and sisters, and the mothers of tomorrow.

"Hence, the forming in our schools, suburban communities, and the like, of a Little Mothers' League. Every girl who joins such a league,—we show them in the initial address made before the girls of the given school for the purpose—is given an official badge. Meetings are held every week, throughout the school year, as well as during the summer; and the members can learn all about how to keep babies well before the season's close.

"Joining the league, we impress on the girls, means that a girl wishes to be helpful and have a part in the greatest service to humanity—that of life-saving.

"With this talk thoroughly 'sent home' to the girls, we distribute pledge cards and arrange the time and the place for the first meeting. There the pledge cards are collected; the members elect their own president and secretary, the latter keeping the pledge cards and recording on each the attendance dates of that member. There follows, then, a short talk on the purpose of the league by the medical inspector of the district; lists of milk stations and relief agencies are distributed, and certificates of membership are made out.

"Further, we then set the order of business for all meetings—call to order by the president, roll-call by the secretary, enrollment of new members, a general discussion of the previous lesson, and then a tenminutes' talk on the subject of the lesson of the day by the inspector, or nurse. There comes, then, a demonstration, by the nurse, of the methods used in subject matter covered by the lessons, this finally closing the meeting, with motion to adjourn.

"With these preparations completed, we are ready for the first lesson. The nurse, or medical inspector, is equipped with a lesson sheet, as it were, giving, in topical form, the subjects to be discussed.

"Lesson I, for example, is devoted to growth and development. First, under this head, is taken up the matter of weight. The average weight of the new-born baby should be about seven pounds. Normally, weight is doubled at the end of six months, up to fourteen pounds. At the end of one year the weight should be three times as much as at birth. Under, or over-weight, on the other hand, does not necessarily mean that anything is wrong, if normal ratio of increase is maintained.

"We then take up the loss of weight in the first few days of life. On the tenth day the baby should weigh as much as at birth. If the breast milk, or artificial feeding, is suited to the baby's needs, gain will be continuous. If no gain by that time, the baby should be taken to the doctor. Baby should be weighed once each week. This can be done at the infant milk stations, if not otherwise.

"We pass from this to muscular development. At three months the baby is generally able to hold up its head. At six, it sits erect, and stands with little support, or alone, at one year. Little mothers are urged not to force the baby to walk. The bones of the legs may be soft (symptoms of rachitis) and bending of the bones of the legs, with permanent deformity, may result.

"From that, attention is taken to the special senses—sight first of all. We show the little girls how, in early life, babies are sensitive to light and should be kept in a semi-dark room during the first few weeks; or, if taken out, should have the eyes protected from strong light. Sunlight should never be permitted to shine directly into the baby's eyes.

"Hearing, then, is dwelt upon—how, after the first few days, the baby's hearing is particularly acute. Loud or sudden noises startle it, and, if often repeated, may cause it to become excited, or even lead to convulsions.

"So, again, speech is considered. We show how a child usually begins to talk at the end of the first year. By the end of the second year, words have been learned. Speech may be delayed, but if the baby cannot talk at all at the end of the second year we emphasize it should be taken to the doctor.

"Teeth make an interesting section of the first lesson. The first teeth, we tell, are twenty in number—ten each in the upper and lower jaws. They appear at about the following ages: Central incisors, 5 to 6 months; lateral, 7 to 8; first molars, 12 to 16; canines, 14 to 20; second molars, 21 to 36th month. The lower set appears, usually, before the upper set. Eruption of these teeth, it is pointed out, may cause the baby to be irritable. If it be sick and teething seems to be the cause, matters should not be neglected and a doctor should be consulted. The first teeth, we likewise urge, must be taken care of. If they are lost too soon, or decay, the jaw becomes misshapen and the second teeth come in crooked and decayed.

"Finally, we show the girls what *especially* to notice in their babies. They should watch the posture when sleeping—how quiet—if limbs be relaxed—if sleep be peaceful, and if there be tossing about. We make them realize that respiration should be regular, easy and quiet, and that the baby should breathe through the nose. The skin should be cool, slightly moist, extremities should be warm. So, again, the facial expression should be calm and peaceful. If the baby is peaceful, it is one thing; if the baby is suffering pain, the features will contract from time to time during sleep!"

So endeth the first lesson!

Then, week by week, the lessons continue.

"The entire second lesson is given over to baths—to the value of water—and how to test it simply;—bran-baths and mustard-baths; powders to be used. Also, the matter of fresh air, indoors and out, and how the little one should be taken to the park or the playground.

"Follows on that a lesson devoted to sleep and quiet. The hours of sleep; the amount of sleep; improvised beds for the poor and how, for one, a barrel hoop may be fastened over the bed, at each end, and covered with a mosquito netting. So as to hammocks, and as to feather-pillows.

"Clothing and cleanliness for summer and winter, making the clothes and the variety of them, take up the fifth lesson entire. The sixth lesson, in its rote, is devoted to first care of the sick baby. Primarily, here, it is emphasized to stop all feeding, to give a dose of castor oil, and then to take the child to a doctor. 'It is easier to keep the baby well than to cure him after he is sick,' is the axiom of this hour.

"An entire lesson for little mothers goes to the subject of milk. Mothers are urged to give the babe the mother's milk, as the natural and best food of all. Substitutes for this are discussed, preparation of cow's milk is taken up, and thus with other lacteal details.

"Lesson VIII has to do with the stomach,—the amount and times of feeding, and such useful don'ts, as not to give the babe sour milk, cold milk, other food than milk or water, and particularly not such things as pickles, lolly-pops, bacon, tea, coffee, beer or ice cream! Then a return is made to milk—the care of the milk in the home and the matter of keeping clean both bottles and nipples. Lesson X develops this still farther, going into the matter of milk modifications, preparation of barley-water and lime-water. The eleventh lesson supplements this with albumen water and other dilutents.

"Finally, at the twelfth meeting, there is a quiz on the subjects covered to date, with essays written on some subjects of the course."

The little girls have taken to the work with avidity, and, proud though they may be of many other things they possess, they take no more pride in any of those than they do in the small, white shield badge that proclaims them of the League of the Little Mothers!

THE SCHOOL AS A SOCIAL SETTLEMENT

Progressives also targeted education for their peculiar brand of reform. In the early twentieth century—as in the early twenty-first century—schools were expected to do more than simply teach children reading, writing, and arithmetic. They were supposed to train good citizens, impart appropriate values and attitudes, provide safe havens from violent neighborhoods, and offer stability and order to children growing up amid the squalor and chaos of urban ghettoes. Schools became, in effect, laboratories for a number of Progressive experiments.

16

JOHN DEWEY AND EVELYN DEWEY

Schools of To-Morrow

1915

The best-known Progressive educator was John Dewey (1859–1952), whose ideas about education influenced several generations of American teachers and educational policy makers. Dewey believed that education must meet the needs of the whole child; rather than simply forcing children into set curricula, schools must engage their students' social, intellectual, emotional, and physical needs and interests. He also argued that schools must not ignore the communities in which they were located. In this excerpt from Schools of To-Morrow *(1915), Dewey (who co-wrote the book with his daughter Evelyn) describes the efforts of one Indianapolis principal to connect a primarily African American elementary school to the community surrounding it, so that it became, in effect, a kind of settlement house (which Dewey refers to as a "social settlement").*

The supervising principal of public school No. 26 in Indianapolis is trying an experiment unlike any other known to us in an effort to make his plant a true school; that is, a place where the children of his neighborhood shall become healthy, happy, and competent both economically and socially, and where the connection of instruction with the life of the community shall be directly recognized both by children and parents. Mr. Valentine's school is located in the poor, crowded

John Dewey and Evelyn Dewey, *Schools of To-Morrow* (New York: E. P. Dutton, 1915), 206–16, 218–21, 223–25.

colored district of the city and has only colored pupils. It is not an attempt to solve the "race question" nor yet an experiment suited only to colored people. There is nothing in the school not entirely practical in any district where the children come from homes with limited resources and meager surroundings. A visitor when leaving this school can not fail to wish that such ventures might be started in all our great cities, — indeed in any community where people need to be aroused to a sense of their needs, including the fact that if they are to contribute to the best interests of the community, they must be taught how to earn a living, and how to use their resources for themselves and their neighbors both in leisure time and in working hours. Mr. Valentine's school is a school for colored children only in the sense that the work has been arranged in relation to the conditions in the neighborhood; these modify the needs of the particular children who are the pupils. Yet the success of the experiment would mean a real step forward in solving the "race question" and peculiar problems of any immigrant district as well. Mr. Valentine is not interested in illustrating any theories on these points, but in making up for gaps in the home life of the pupils; giving them opportunities to prepare for a better future; in supplying plenty of healthy occupation and recreation; and in seeing to it that their school work reacts at once to improve neighborhood conditions. . . .

The neighborhood around Mr. Valentine's school is one of the poorest in Indianapolis, and once had a bad reputation for lawlessness and disorder as well. The school had struggled along for years with little or no support from the community as a whole or from individual parents. The per cent. of truancy was high, and a large number of cases were sent to the juvenile court each year. The children took no interest in their work as a whole, and cases of extreme disorder were not infrequent; one pupil tried to revenge himself on his teacher for a merited punishment with a butcher's knife, in another case it was necessary to arrest a boy's father as a lesson to the neighborhood. Besides this attitude of hostility and of unwilling attendance, the school had to contend with immoral surroundings which finally made it necessary to do something to isolate the school building from neighboring houses. Finally the school board bought the tract of land and wooden tenements around the school building. It was at first proposed to tear down the old buildings, but the authorities were persuaded to turn them over to the school for its use. The school now found itself the possessor of a large playground and of three frame tenements in the worst possible condition, the board having stipulated that this added property should mean no further expense to the city after its purchase and the cleaning up of the grounds. It was decided to use the buildings for social and industrial purposes. One of them was fitted up by the pupils and neighbors interested as a manual training building. In this there is a carpenter shop, a sewing room, and a room for the class in shoemaking. Each grade devotes a regular number of hours a week to hand work, and has an opportunity to join other industrial classes after school. The immediate practical appeal of the work is never lost sight of, and the work is arranged to fit the needs of the individual pupil.

The carpenter shop is open all day, and there are classes for the girls as well as for the boys. Pupils are at liberty to go into the shop and work whenever they have any free time. The work is not confined to exercises to train the child in the use of tools, but each pupil makes something that he needs or wants, something that will be of real use to him. Processes and control of tools are taught the pupil by means of the piece of work he is doing. This is the keynote to all the industrial work done in the school. The more remote end of teaching the child processes which will be useful to him later is not lost sight of, but material is always used which has some immediate value to the child or to the school. The boys have learned carpentry work by making things that were needed in the school building—tables, cupboards, and bookcases—and by doing some of the repairing on the building. The girls have learned to sew by making clothes for themselves, for their brothers and sisters, and by making curtains and linen for the school. They have learned to cook by making soup for hot lunches for the school and the neighbors, and by cooking a whole meal for their own class. Besides the cooking and sewing department for the girls, there is a class in millinery and in crocheting. These two classes are conducted from the commercial point of view, to teach the girls to do something that will enable them to earn some money. In the millinery class the pupils start by making and trimming hats for themselves, so that they learn the different processes in the trade. The girls in the class who show the most skill are then allowed to take orders from friends and neighbors and trim or make hats for them. Besides the cost of the material the buyer pays a very small sum for the work, and this goes into the school treasury. The millinery class has done quite a business in the neighborhood, and turned out some very successful hats. Crocheting is taught as a trade, and any girl who wishes to make some money has an opportunity to learn how to make lace, table doilies, and all sorts of crocheted articles, like hoods, etc., which will sell. As the girls are learning, they are working on something which they can use for themselves or in their homes.

The work for the boys is arranged in the same way. Besides the carpenter work and the repairing there is a boys' cooking class, a shoe-repairing department, and a tailoring shop. The cooking class is even more popular with the boys than with the girls. In the shoe-repairing shop, which holds classes after school hours, the boys learn to mend their own shoes. A professional cobbler is the teacher, and the mending must be neatly done. The boys begin work on their own old shoes and as they progress in skill, are allowed to bring shoes from home to be repaired, or to mend for the girls and for the younger boys in the school, who, however, pay a small sum for the work. The tailoring department is run on the same plan, to teach habits of personal neatness and of industry through giving the pupils work that results in neatness and gives some manual skill and control of tools. The class is taught by a tailor, and the boys learn to patch and mend their own clothes, as well as to sponge and press them. Attendance is entirely voluntary, and the class meets after the regular school work is over. Knowing how to keep themselves tidy has resulted in a very marked improvement in the appearance and habits of the boys in the class, and has had an influence not only on the whole school, but on the neighborhood as well. The boys no longer resent the attempts of the teachers to influence them towards cleanliness and neatness, for they have become conscious of the advantages of these habits.

The cooking and domestic science classes are taught in one of the tenements turned over to the school without having been repaired, although the cooking equipment was supplied by the city. All the other work on the building—cleaning, painting, repairing, furnishing, and decorating—was done and paid for by the pupils of the school with help from the neighborhood clubs that use the building. There is a large cooking room, a demonstration dining and sitting room, and two bedrooms. The girls not only learn to cook real meals, but they learn how to serve them, and then how to take care of the demonstration house. The domestic science classes include lessons in buying, the comparative costs and values of food, something of food chemistry and values, and large quantity cooking. This work is done in connection with the soup kitchen. A group of girls have charge of the kitchen long enough to really learn about the work. They plan the menu and do the buying, cooking and serving of the soup, selling it for three cents a bowl to the pupils of the school and to neighbors. They keep all the accounts and not only have to make all their expenses, but are expected to make some profit for the use of the school as well. They have made enough profit in one year to furnish most of the demonstration house. Aside from teaching how to do housework thoroughly and easily, the purpose of the house is to furnish an example of what can be done to make one of the regular frame tenements of the district comfortable and attractive, without more expense than most of the people now put into their homes. The house is very simply furnished, with cheap and strong things, in plain colors that are easily kept clean; the painting and papering was done by the pupils. The sewing class has made all the curtains and linen for the house, and made furniture by covering boxes, etc. Besides the class work that goes on in the building, the rooms are also used as a social center for the girls of the school.

The third building left standing on the ground purchased by the school authorities has been turned into a boys' club house. There is a gymnasium, two club rooms, and a shower bath room. This house was in exceedingly bad condition when it became part of the school property, and there was no money and not much lumber available to repair it. But the boys of the school wanted the club house, and were not discouraged because it was not given to them all finished. They started out, as they had done in the manual training and domestic science buildings, to do the work themselves. Under the direction of the manual training teacher, they pulled off old paper and broken plaster, tore up uneven floors and took out partitions. Then they laid floors, put in woodwork and painted it, rehung doors, mended windows, and made furniture and gymnastic apparatus. When there was a job they could not do, such as the plastering and plumbing, they went among their friends and asked for money or help in work. Plumbers and plasterers who lived near the school came in and gave their time and work to help the boys get their building in order, and other friends gave enough money to finish the work. Men in the neighborhood dug a long ditch through the school grounds for sewerage connections. Gradually they are adding to the gymnasium apparatus and to the simple bathing facilities, while cleaning and keeping up the painting continue to supply opportunities for useful work. . . .

The school is also carrying on definite work to arouse the pupils to a sense of responsibility for their community and neighbors. Giving the pupils as much liberty and responsibility as possible around the school buildings is an important factor. Each pupil in the higher grades is given some small child in one of the lower grades to look out for. On the playground they see to it that the charge has a fair chance to play, and that he behaves himself; they see that the little boy or girl comes to school clean and tidy, if necessary doing the washing or mending themselves. This work has proved especially successful in doing away with bullying and in arousing personal pride and a sense of responsibility in the older children; the younger ones are better looked after than before and have many opportunities to learn things from the older and more advanced pupils. The older pupils are also encouraged in every way to help in carrying on the outside activities of the school. They make calls and write notes to keep up the attendance at the night school; they see to the order of the principal's office and keep the boys' club house in order. All the teachers of the school are agreed upon a policy of frank discussion of the poverty of the district, and of urging the pupils to earn money to help their parents by becoming as nearly self-supporting as possible. Each grade keeps track of what its members earn and how they earn it, and the grade with the largest sum to its credit feels that it has accomplished something worth while during the year.

There is a savings bank in the school to teach the children habits of thrift and economy; here a pupil may deposit any sum from a penny up. The pupil receives a bank book in which stamps are pasted for his deposits, the money being kept in a city savings bank. The school also has a branch library, and the pupils are taught how to use it. Part of the playground has been made into a school garden, and here every pupil in the higher grades has a garden plot, also instruction which enables him to grow successfully some of the commoner fruits and flowers. This work is made very practical; the children have the sort of garden that would be useful and ornamental if it were in their own back yard. The school carries on a neighborhood campaign for home gardens, and the pupils with school gardens do much of this work, telling the people who want gardens what to plant, and giving them practical help with their plot until it is well established. In all these ways the teachers are trying to make ambitious, responsible citizens out of the student body. Inside the school pupils are taught higher standards of living than prevail in their homes, and they are taught as well trades and processes which will at least give them a start towards prosperity, and then, too, they are aroused to a feeling of responsibility for the welfare of the whole community. . . .

The pupils of the school are given social as well as educational opportunities through their school life. The boys' club house is opened nearly every night to local boys' clubs, some of them being school organizations and some independent ones. There are rooms for the boys to hold meetings and to play games, and a well-equipped gymnasium. The teachers of the school take turns supervising these evening gatherings. The attendance is large for the size of the building. Giving the boys a place for wholesome activities has done much to break up the habits of street loafing and the gangs which were so common in the district. The girls of the school use the domestic science house for social purposes. Two chapters of the Camp Fire girls hold regular meetings in the building and get help and advice from the teachers. Each domestic science class aims to teach the girls how to live a comfortable and self-respecting life, as well as how to do housework, and so becomes a social center of its own. The girls learn to cook and serve good cheap meals, and then they sit down together and eat what they have cooked. They talk over their individual problems with the teacher and with each other, and give each other much practical help. The domestic science teacher helps the girls who have some skill find work to do after school hours so that they can help their families by helping themselves; she helps the pupils find steady work as they leave school and then keeps track of them, encouraging them to go on fitting themselves for better work.

The success of the settlement work the school has done points strongly to the fact that the schoolhouse is the natural and logical social center in a neighborhood, the teachers coming into closer and more natural contact with both children and parents than is possible in the case of other district workers.

There are large economies combining the school and the settlement in districts where the social and economic standards of living are so low that the people are not especially successful citizens. Both the school and settlement facilities are enlarged by using the same group of buildings for both purposes. The settlement has the use of better and larger shops and classrooms than most settlements can command, and the school uses the social rooms and activities to become itself a community. The school comes in contact with almost all the families in a district so that community action is much easier to establish. But even more important than these economies are the far-reaching results which come from the fact that the school settlement is a democratic community, really reflecting the conditions of the community.

————

JUVENILE JUSTICE

When families fell apart, when school was perceived as a dead end, when the social outlets that society offered were unsatisfying, when the temptations of city streets became too great—in short, when all of the inhibitions and safeguards that normally prevented girls and boys from breaking laws and breeching social customs failed—children and youth inevitably ran afoul of the law and of their elders. They fought on city streets, stole from shopkeepers, gambled in dark alleys, associated with prostitutes, violated curfews, talked back to teachers and their parents, and engaged in illicit sex. Any of these offenses— some of which violated actual laws, some of which only violated adults' perceptions of proper behavior—could end with a trip to one of the juvenile courts that were charged not only with upholding the law but also with maintaining community order.

17

BENJAMIN B. LINDSEY

The Dangerous Life
1931

Although the first juvenile court in the United States was established in Cook County (Chicago), Illinois, the judge most closely associated with the movement to create a separate juvenile justice system was Benjamin B. Lindsey, who used the existing Colorado "school law" to pull child defendants out of adult courts. His approach—a combination of family therapy, commonsense problem solving, and middle-class paternalism—became the model for many juvenile court judges nationwide. The following excerpt from one of his books describes his first encounter, as a young lawyer, with child defendants occupying jail cells with hardened criminals. The episode, which took place in the 1890s, would inspire his missionary-like zeal for bringing justice and compassion to juvenile defendants.

The clerk gave me the numbers of the cases. I got the pleadings [court case paperwork] and went into the old West Side jail to see my clients. The Warden smiled when I told him their names. I followed

Benjamin B. Lindsey and Rube Borough, *The Dangerous Life* (New York: Horace Liveright, Inc., 1931), 49–52.

him through clanging iron doors with their rattling bolts and bars to the back part of the building.

At the end of a corridor I came in front of a cage on the floor of which were two small boys engaged in gambling with two grown men who had been brought in from some outlying section of Arapahoe county, a sparsely settled empire that then ran clear to the eastern state line.

I found that these boys had already been in jail more than 60 days and had learned to play poker from their older cell mates, a safe cracker and a horse thief, upon whom they had come to look as great heroes.

My first thought was that the judge in assigning me to defend two such men from serious crimes had given me a pretty tough job but my concern was soon relieved as the Warden explained:

"It's the kids the judge wants you to look after. He was over here the other day and he didn't like it very much that they're still here. He said he knew a young fellow who was just the one to look after the case. I guess it must be you."

"Then," I asked, to make doubly sure, "it's not those two men who are my clients?"

"No," he drawled. "Those guys have got two real lawyers to defend 'em."

"But," I persisted, "I am appointed to defend two burglars."

The kids looked like such real boys that in my confusion I had been unable to visualize them as criminals—my mind just refused to work that way.

"Sure you are," said the Warden, "but them's the burglars."

A number of things shot through my mind as this first step in my difficulties cleared up. One was that it, perhaps, took "two burglars" like these boys to make "one burglar." And so my pride that had soared from the flattery of two assignments when any young fellow would have been tickled to death with one was a bit humbled.

My first task—that was afterward to become my task in so many thousands of cases that I then little knew were to follow—was to get acquainted with the prisoners. It was my first appearance before the bench of youth but its lesson was to stay with me even in the days when I had long ceased to be a lawyer and had become a judge. For there by those bars that would have shamed the King Tiger of the Jungle I was able to begin a lasting friendship with the little prisoners.

They were typical boys from the realm of Gangville, as I was to come to know it so well. They were about twelve years of age.

The one that impressed me most was a little freckle-faced Irish lad with a sense of humor. He was charged with having gone into a railroad section house and taken a lot of tools.

"Sonny," I said, "you are charged with burglary."

"I ain't no burglary," he countered.

"I guess you don't know what burglary means," I ventured. And I explained to him that the long rigamarole in the complaint papers meant to charge him with breaking and entering a tool house and *that* constituted burglary.

"I never stole 'em, I just took 'em," he answered heatedly. "So I ain't done no burglary—I ain't done nothin'."

"Well, one thing you can't deny," I went on, getting chummy with my client. "You've got the dirtiest face I ever saw on a kid."

"'Tain't my fault," he shot back with a grin. "A guy threw water on me and the dust settled on it."

When I protested to the Warden against this good-natured boy being held in jail with two hardened old criminals, he admitted it was "a damned outrage."

"How many boys are there in jail?" I asked.

"Oh, quite a number," he answered. "Most of them don't stay so long as these two boys—they're waiting for the fall term of court. Their families couldn't afford to put up bonds."

"But why do you put them in with that horse thief and safe cracker?"

"The jail is crowded," he said. And he gave various other excuses.

Well, in answering the charge against those kids, I did a thing that was perhaps purely artless, the direct reaction from my rage complexes, my indignation at injustice.

I prepared an answer that was an indictment against the state of Colorado for its crime against those two boys. The thing got a lot of public discussion and raised quite a furor.

Here were two boys, neither of them serious enemies of society, who were about to be convicted of burglary and have felony records standing against them for the remainder of their lives. And, pending the decision of their cases, they were associating generally with criminals and particularly with a horse thief and a safe cracker. The state was sending them to a school for crime—deliberately teaching them to be horse thieves and safe crackers. It was outrageous—and absurd.

My first fight then was with the state of Colorado. I was determined that those boys should have their chance. I saw only vaguely then what afterward became clearer to me—that my first fight with the state was not just for those two boys but for millions like them. Even then, however,—before I had formulated any plan to change the things that were or had written any of the hundreds of laws I afterward wrote for my own and other states and foreign countries—I had made up my mind to smash the system that meant so much injustice to youth.

18

HELEN RANKIN JETER

The Chicago Juvenile Court

1922

More than twenty years after Lindsey and other reformers began establishing juvenile court systems, the United States Children's Bureau published a report on the Chicago juvenile court. Excerpts from that report show how the sympathetic and often informal treatment of juveniles envisioned by Lindsey had been standardized and bureaucratized over the years, especially in the "detention home." In addition, the case studies of children's experiences with the court and other child welfare agencies highlight the daunting problems facing the needy children who came before the court as well as officials' concerns with the immoral, not only illegal, activities of juveniles.

Reception of Children

When a child is admitted to the home, important facts regarding the case are recorded. The child is then taken to the graduate nurse, who records temperature, pulse, and respiration, takes a throat culture, swabs the throat with an antiseptic solution, and administers a grain of

Helen Rankin Jeter, *The Chicago Juvenile Court* (Washington, D.C.: U.S. Government Printing Office, 1922), 54–56, 66–67.

calomel, followed by magnesium sulphate.[1] If the child is a girl, an examination for gonorrhea is made as a protection to the other inmates. A shampoo and antiseptic bath are given, and the child is dressed in detention-home clothes, so that its own may be sent to the fumigator.

The house physician is on duty every morning except Sunday and examines each child who has been admitted during the previous 24 hours. The doctor's findings and recommendations are recorded on a card which accompanies the child to court and is given to the judge, who advises the parents if the child needs medical care and obtains their signature if they consent to carry out the recommendations.

As a precaution against the spread of disease all children are kept in the receiving wards after admission to the home until the result of the doctor's examination and the throat and vaginal cultures is known. This period of isolation is usually from 24 to 48 hours. Most medical and surgical cases, including all gonorrheal infections and cases of ringworm of the scalp, are sent to the county hospital for treatment. Certain contagious diseases and some kinds of eye, ear, nose, and throat trouble are treated in the isolation rooms of the home.

As a precaution against the spread of contagion the one or two days that the children are kept under observation in the receiving wards are inadequate. The incubation period of acute contagious disease is from one day to three weeks, but owing to cramped quarters, particularly downstairs in the receiving wards, the children are allowed to go upstairs as soon as their cultures are reported on, providing there is no evidence of disease.

The attending physicians have repeatedly stressed the fact that better isolation facilities should be provided for sick children. In 1917 the home had within its walls 190 cases of acute tonsillitis, 42 of pharyngitis, 45 of impetigo, 68 of venereal disease, 22 of ringworm, 24 of scabies, 3 of trachoma, as well as a few very severe cases of pediculosis and 141 diphtheria carriers, all demanding rigid quarantine. In 1918, cases of sickness among its inmates numbered 1,650. Thus the request for a separate small hospital building does not seem unreasonable.

The teeth of all children kept in the home over 48 hours are examined, except in the cases of positive throat cultures. A record is made of conditions found and of all work done. So far as possible in the limited time children are under detention, defects are remedied, and the

---

[1]Calomel, also called mercury oxide, was often used as a laxative. Magnesium sulphate, called epsom salt when mixed with water, was also used as a laxative.

children are taught to care for their teeth. The dentist's services are provided only 18 hours a week, and a great deal more work is needed than can be accomplished in that short time.

The Daily Routine

Much of the work in their own sections is done by the children themselves, thus:

> The delinquent children do practically all of the work in their own departments. They rise at 5 a.m., turn back their bedding, throw the windows open, and begin their daily duties. They scrub almost their entire department before breakfast, which is at 6:45 a.m. Immediately after breakfast they clear their tables, wash the dishes, and tea towels, scrub the dining room and make their beds. At 9 a.m., when the work is usually completed, they wash, comb their hair, and change their clothes, ready for school at 9:30 a.m. The girls, besides doing the work in their own section, assist in the preparation of the vegetables and wash the employees' dishes. They also scrub the dormitories of the dependent section and assist in making the beds of that department. The boys scrub the main hall of the dependent section and the kitchen. If at any time the girls are under quarantine, the boys are detailed to the kitchen work.

After these strenuous hours the children spend from 9:30 to 12 and from 1:20 to 4 in school. Children under 10 years of age are cared for in a group by themselves, and their work is informal and social. The kindergarten room for little dependents is particularly attractive. Visiting and recreation hours are from 4 to 5 p.m. and from 7 to 8 p.m. Parents may visit the children during these hours five days a week. The boys play outdoors in the court under supervision, but the girls have no outdoor recreation. Time hangs heavy on the hands of the children under observation in the receiving rooms, inasmuch as they can neither go to school nor play outdoors and have no one to direct their play in the house.

The children are entertained every Friday evening with music, lectures, stereopticon views [slide shows], and aesthetic dancing, and a special entertainment is always provided on holidays. Occasionally the downtown theaters present the home with tickets for some suitable play. Religious instruction is furnished for both Catholic and Protestant children by outside religious organizations.

Discipline is usually left to the nurses in charge. Under no circumstances is corporal punishment resorted to, but occasionally when special severity seems needed, children are put on a bread-and-milk diet and sometimes they are placed in solitary confinement for an hour or two "to think it over." . . .

The following cases, while few in number, illustrate situations that are typical of many situations with which the court deals through this device:

Virginia D., aged 15, was brought into court by her mother. She had been keeping late hours in bad company, and one night stayed out until 2 a.m. The case was continued for seven months under the supervision of the district officer.

October 27, 1919: First hearing. Virginia working without a certificate. Disobedient and defiant. To live at home under supervision.

November 7, 1919: Probation officer visited. Virginia had obtained a work certificate. Was doing office work and going to night school.

November 26, 1919: Case in court. Virginia had stayed away from home all night. Found in park next morning. Said she had ridden round on street cars all night. Given another chance at home.

December 2, 1919: Probation officer reports home conditions poor, but Virginia behaving better.

January 19, 1920: Virginia left home. Family learned that she was staying with a family in Geneva, Ill., who were at first willing to keep her, but a month later sent her home, as they did not wish to be responsible for her.

March 29, 1920: Case in court. Virginia working and causing no trouble. Continued to April 23, 1920.

April 2, 1920: Probation officer visited. Virginia working.

April 16, 1920: Virginia admits she has not been working for a week. Mother can not manage her.

April 23, 1920: Case in court. Virginia again working. Has lied about her age to employer and is not going to night school. Case continued.

May 20, 1920: Virginia ran away from home. Picked up by the police and taken to the detention home.

June 2, 1920: Case in court. Virginia had been unmanageable in detention home. Placed under supervision of child-placing division to live at M. E. Club.

June 30, 1920: Case in court. Virginia had run away from club and had been immoral. Probation officer on case stated that she had never seen the girl. Committed to the House of the Good Shepherd.

Harriet L., a colored girl, aged 17. Mother dead, father married again. Stepmother complained that girl had stolen money from her father and had torn up her stepmother's clothing. Case continued five months.

December 30, 1919: First hearing. Evidences of mental defect, but father and probation officer have been unable to get her to the psychopathic institute for an examination. Case continued to January 6, 1920.

January 6, 1920: Case in court. Continued for a warrant, as girl refuses to come to court or to have psychopathic examination.

January 21, 1920: Case in court. Continued for report of examination.

January 28, 1920: Case in court. Psychopathic institute reports that Harriet is neither feeble-minded nor insane, but has very peculiar reactions. Girl complains of stepmother's treatment. Willing to try working in a private home. Continued under supervision of district officer. To be placed in private home.

February 2, 1920: Case set for hearing before Judge Arnold to confirm assistant's recommendation. No one present. Continued.

February 21, 1920: Placed in working girls' home. Matron refused to keep her because she was so slovenly. Discharged from laundry because too slow.

March 11, 1920: Placed in another family. Probation officer visited once. Found that Harriet was doing day work and was dirty and untidy. Her father had given her money for clothes. A friend of hers was interviewed a month later, but the girl was not seen.

June 4, 1920: Case in court. No one but probation officer present. Girl was then 18. No improvement was reported, but the case was continued generally.

Irene T., aged 13. Neighbors complained of her conduct and case was brought to court by police probation officer. Continued eight months.

June 10, 1919: First hearing. Girl had been out of school. Neighbors had complained that she was often alone in the house with a man who, according to her mother, was a friend of her brother's. Mother refused to allow a medical examination, but had a satisfactory statement from her own doctor. Case continued, with no order for supervision.

June 27, 1919: Case in court. Truant officer testifies that absence from school accounted for illness. Mother objects to suggestion of sending her to a convalescent home. Case continued.

Case in court four times between June 27, 1919, and January 6, 1920. Each time mother failed to appear, and the case was continued.

January 6, 1920: Case in court. Irene had given birth to a child on Christmas day. A few weeks before this the mother had had her married at the city hall by giving her age as 16. She had paid a doctor $2 to give her the statement presented to the court at the first hearing. Case continued.

January 20, 1920: Case in court. Irene complains that she was forced to give the child to her sister-in-law for adoption. Continuance one week to investigate the matter.

January 27, 1920: Case in court. Irene to live at home. Child to remain with aunt. Marriage has been annulled. Irene's brother undertakes to see that she does not live with the man again until she is 16 and can be legally married. Case dismissed.

Richard R. was a dependent boy 9 years old. His parents were divorced, and his mother worked as a housemaid in a private family. He had been under the court's jurisdiction since 1918 and had been placed in several homes. In 1919 his custodian complained of his bad habits and stealing and refused to keep him any longer. The case was brought to court for rehearing in February, 1919, and was continued seven times during a period of nine months, ending in dismissal.

February 24, 1919: Case in court. Probation officer requests continuance to see what she can do with child.

March 12, 1919: Case in court. Temporary home found by Illinois Children's Home and Aid Society. Continued.

March 12, 1919: Case in court. Probation officer has found home. Continued.

March 31, 1919: Case in court. Report that child is provided for until September. Continued.

July 2, 1919: Case in court. Report that child is provided for until September. Continued.

September 8, 1919: Case in court. No one present. Continued.

September 17, 1919: Case in court. Boy so attached to custodian that arrangement prolonged until January.

January 6, 1920: Case in court. No one present. Continued.

January 19, 1920: Case in court. Custodian wishes to keep child. Case dismissed.

The record contains no report of any visit to this family or of the conditions in the home. It is probable that the home was approved by the Illinois Children's Home and Aid Society.

"THE DAY OF THE CHILD HAS COME": THE CHICAGO CHILD WELFARE EXHIBIT, 1911

The Chicago Child Welfare Exhibit, held May 11–25, 1911, exemplified Progressive efforts to inform and advocate on behalf of children. Held in the Chicago Coliseum, just south of downtown during a late spring heat wave, the exhibit was funded by Mr. and Mrs. Cyrus H. McCormick, who had long been involved in child welfare philanthropy. The exhibit consisted of scores of booths and displays, as well as a series of conferences featuring most of the nation's leading child welfare experts.

Each day featured a specific theme: "Libraries and Museums," "Mother's Day," "The Colored Child," "The Foreign Child," "Clubs and Associations," "Sunday School Day," "The Working Child," or "The Child at Play." The speakers tackled children's issues from birth through adolescence: prenatal and infant health care, clean water and pasteurized milk, better nutrition and designs for nursery furniture, visiting nurses and baby clinics, social workers and pediatricians, playground administration and educational toys, artistic and vocational education, "dependent" children (orphans and children with disabilities) and foster care, boys clubs, and juvenile courts. Private organizations, public schools, government agencies, and many other philanthropic groups mounted displays and exhibits or sent representatives to the program. The Chicago public school district set up model classrooms, where observers could see methods for training deaf, blind, and crippled students; girls demonstrated cooking and sewing; and boys demonstrated printing and binding techniques.

The displays featured photographs, posters, charts, and hands-on presentations organized into three sections: the home, public programs, and private philanthropy. Visitors first strolled through a series of displays related to the home life of children, from clothes and nutrition to toys and sandboxes, from simple, child-friendly furnishings to proper ventilation, and from housekeeping techniques to personal hygiene. To the left of the home section was the Civics section, with displays on organizations and efforts sponsored by state and local governments. To the right, in the Philanthropy section, were displays on those institutions and programs funded by private sponsors.

Although displays relied heavily on posters, hands-on demonstrations (including wax models of healthy and sick children to illustrate the effects of poor and good nutrition), and objects (furniture, toys, and medical equipment), a few of the booths made their points graphically. The most dramatic exhibit consisted of three thousand dolls revolving on a cylinder, with a scythe—the implement carried by the specter of death in popular illustrations—looming overhead; occasionally the scythe fell, dropping a doll into a bin. Each fallen toy represented one of the infants who needlessly died in Chicago every year.

The exhibit drew huge crowds throughout its two-week run. Between 20,000 and 45,000 people streamed into the Coliseum every day, and by the time a lone Boy Scout played taps on his bugle to close the exhibit at the end of the two weeks, more than 416,000 people had attended.

19

CYRUS H. McCORMICK

Introductory Remarks

1911

Mr. and Mrs. Cyrus H. McCormick funded the Chicago Child Welfare Exhibit. The McCormicks were known for their philanthropy on behalf of children, which they dedicated to the memory of their daughter Elizabeth, who had died in 1905 at the age of twelve. Mr. McCormick's opening remarks—especially his dramatic assertion that "the march of progress will begin with those who bring betterment into the lives of children"—reveal the outrage as well as the hopefulness that characterized much of the exhibit and the child welfare movement as a whole.

A great educator has said, "There is nothing in all the world so important as children—nothing so interesting."

If mankind is to be reformed or improved, we must begin with the child. This Exhibit has been organized to show what has already been done for children, and to demonstrate the importance and the necessity of doing much more along this line.

Cyrus H. McCormick, *The Child in the City: A Handbook of the Child Welfare Exhibit at the Coliseum, May 11 to May 25, 1911* (Chicago: Blakely Printing Co., 1911), 1–3.

In my capacity of assistant to your Honorary President, I have been asked to preside at this meeting, and in so doing let me first thank Miss Addams, Mr. Kingsley, and all the committees for their devoted and enthusiastic labors which have brought this undertaking, in so short a time, to this splendid fulfillment. It is inspiring to see one thousand people giving their time and strength to the work of these committees and spreading the message of welfare to the helpless and undeveloped child.

Chicago is now to be given an opportunity to study child life in all its various phases. Here will be seen the latest steps in progressive educational efforts for children, as well as the vitally important needs of sanitation and of housing conditions to protect the child's life and health. The needs of children are being intelligently considered today as never before by parents, doctors and scientists; and this Exhibit will show that this investigation is not merely the work of the doctrinaire and the visionary, but that it is rational and practical.

The city tenement robs the child of his birthright of pure air, of pleasant and wholesome play, and of appropriate work. What advantages in return does the community afford for instructing the child as he grows up, and training him for a useful life-work? Do the laws sufficiently provide for the protection of the inherent and essential rights of childhood? The wise care of its children is one of the highest duties of the State. Those who enjoy the benefits and share the responsibilities of our cities must plan for the children, for, although they are our youngest citizens, they are potentially the most important. The city that cares most for its children will be the greatest city.

Human life is sacred because the individual lives it but once, and society has but one chance to benefit from it. We are told that three hundred thousand children die annually in this country. A large proportion of these deaths, perhaps one-half, are due, not to unavoidable conditions, but to ignorance. Physicians and philanthropists, after careful observation, agree that the prevention of infant mortality depends upon the earnest, united and continued effort of intelligent and capable men and women.

The child carries the burdens of heredity, environment, parental influence, lack of play, insufficient food; of poverty, sorrow, sin, and all the economic and social influences which have affected his parents. We shall see in this Exhibit—as perhaps we have never realized before—the sadness of child life, and if we ask ourselves the question, "What can be done about it," we shall learn that wise men and women have given us the answer and are showing us how we can meet these needs; how we can lift the burden from the backs of the little children, and receive our reward in their smiling faces.

This Child Welfare Exhibit will surely lead to definite things, and when, in future years, we can realize our hopes, and the child of the congested districts shall have better hygienic surroundings; when the efforts of humanity shall have overcome the "White Plague" [tuberculosis]; when school life and home life shall conduce to better and more normal development of our children, then may we realize a new era for the community of "children of a larger growth." The march of progress will begin with those who bring betterment into the lives of children, and "a little child shall lead them."

20

CHICAGO CHILD WELFARE EXHIBIT

Team Work for City Boys

1911

Child welfare reformers were particularly concerned about boys: their needs, their desires, their capacity for mischief, their tendency to form "gangs," their untapped potential for good. The boys' section of the Child Welfare Exhibit featured many different agencies and organizations designed to channel boys' boundless energy—their "animal spirits," in the words of one poster—so they could become orderly, self-reliant, useful citizens.

"Just because a boy bubbles with animal spirits, boils over with mischief, does a few things that are bad, he is not necessarily a 'bad boy.' Boys cooped up must be given the chance to study, to have fun, to be fair, to understand team play, to learn to be useful, to develop self-reliance and civic pride." So runs the inscription on one of the first screens in the Child Welfare Exhibit. It strikes a keynote—belief in the boy, and determination that he shall have fair treatment.

The Child in the City: A Handbook of the Child Welfare Exhibit at the Coliseum, May 11 to May 25, 1911 (Chicago: Blakely Printing Co., 1911), 8–11.

The gang spirit, as every friend of children knows, is a marked characteristic of boys growing up. In every street and alley you find them, playing ball, pegging tops, wrestling, talking over the latest news or nickel show, but always in groups and sharing the same group life. This gang instinct, which many a policeman has encountered and many a mother has opposed in vain, is a crude expression of the spirit of association and co-operation upon which the work presented in the Associations and Clubs' section is built. Organized and directed, the gang becomes the boys' club. It helps him to secure his rights, but makes a clear distinction between "right rights" and "wrong rights."

In Chicago there are 25,000 boys in recognized clubs. They meet for many purposes—athletic, educational, recreational, social. The occasions are many, but the final aim is one—to satisfy the craving for companionship in work and play. The boys' clubs of the Y.M.C.A. [Young Men's Christian Association] have a four-fold aim, which is brought out strongly in both the Chicago and New York exhibits. They plan for the boy's development along physical, social, educational and spiritual lines. There are 3,500 boys in the clubs under the direction of the Chicago Y.M.C.A. One-half of these are members of the Association; the others are not members, but are brought in through some form of extension work. Often this is simply free membership in the regular club.

Entering these clubs, a boy receives first of all a physical examination. Trained directors look him over to determine whether he is able to take all the regular gymnasium work, to discover bodily weaknesses and to prescribe special exercises to correct these. A swimming pool is an adjunct of most of the Y.M.C.A. gymnasiums, and swimming classes are doing much to overcome what is almost a national deficiency. In fact, the Y.M.C.A. is conducting a country-wide campaign to cut down the annual total of 4,000 drownings. Last year, something like 31,000 boys and young men were taught to take care of themselves in the water.

"Hikes" to the country are part of the club programs during autumn, winter and spring. During the summer, vacation camps give hundreds of boys two weeks or more in the country and the contact with nature which every city boy needs. The serious side of club work is represented by classes for educational and religious purposes in the winter. Even in the summer camps, this class work is part of the program.

More picturesque, and by reason of their phenomenal progress more interesting at the moment, are the "Boy Scouts of America."

Though the movement is only a little more than a year old in the United States, its membership has almost reached the half-million mark, and its ideals and activities promise to touch and influence more boys than any other movement launched in this country. Chicago has 4,350 boy scouts organized in one hundred and twenty-one companies, with one hundred and fifteen men as scout masters and nearly four hundred and fifty boys as patrol leaders.

"A scout is a friend to all and a brother to every other scout." "A scout's honor is to be trusted." "A scout's duty is to be useful and to help others." These and other commandments of the scout law which explain the aims and ideals of the organization are displayed in the exhibit. The scout's pledge is also given:

"On my honor, I promise to do my best,
To do my duty to God and my country,
To help other people at all times,
To obey the Scout law."

The training of a boy scout includes a hundred experiences of which a city life and environment rob the average boy. There are afternoon "hikes" to the country, overnight camps and week-end camps, at which the scouts pitch their tents, light fires and cook food under the direction of the scout master. They learn woodcraft. They learn to steer a course through strange country by the sun and stars. They learn to know trees, plants, flowers and animals as even the country boy does not know them. They learn to observe closely, to analyze, to remember important circumstances. They develop initiative. Before a boy can win the badge of a first-class scout, he must have proved his ability to do and endure in difficult situations. Character-building is the chief aim, but the intelligence is not neglected.

21

CHICAGO CHILD WELFARE EXHIBIT

Child Health and Welfare

1911

Programs and agencies dedicated to children's health dominated the Child Welfare Exhibit. Virtually every booth, poster, demonstration, and lecture related in some way to improving children's chances for surviving to adulthood. The following selections from the exhibit catalog show reformers' efforts to educate readers and visitors about the most recent medical treatments; to advocate the rejection of "old" ways of caring for children in favor of new, more scientific methods; and to suggest a few of the ways in which local governments, with relatively little expense, could dramatically improve the health of city children.

Child health is the general text and inspiration of the whole Welfare Exhibit. Hardly a section but contributes something towards solving the problem of giving every baby born a better chance of living and growing up, a surer title to strength, happiness and usefulness. But the Health section has no other end or aim except to show what the city and a score of philanthropic agencies are doing to correct the handicaps and dangers so many Chicago children are born to; and to point out to the community and to individual fathers and mothers how much remains to be done and how to do it.

Thirty-five hundred children died in Chicago last year from preventable diseases. No more pathetic array of dolls was ever assembled than that with which the Health Department, in one of its rooms, illustrates the army of little citizens who had to fall out of the ranks before life's march was fairly begun. They carry the colors of the enemy that overcame them—scarlet fever, diphtheria, meningitis, stomach troubles, tuberculosis and other deadly ills. They are there as grim reminders that the child-saving work of the community, though well begun, is not one-half, or one-tenth done. The entire Health section is

---

The Child in the City: A Handbook of the Child Welfare Exhibit at the Coliseum, May 11 to May 25, 1911 (Chicago: Blakely Printing Co., 1911), 46–58.

no more than a big object lesson demonstrating what can be done, what must be done before Chicago's children all get a fair chance at life and what it holds for each of them.

Broadly considered, the Health section divides itself into three groups of exhibits: *first,* those illustrating the organized efforts of philanthropic men and women to meet the problems of child-saving in the child's own home; *second,* the efficient but still limited work of the City Health Department to correct blighting conditions and spread the gospel of pure air, proper food and the prevention of contagious diseases; *third,* the work of the various children's hospitals and dispensaries—the institutional side of the growing campaign against the crippling and destroying influences in city life. This classification is only general; one group merges into another. While as background for the splendid Chicago showing is the remarkable series of thirty-nine screens covering like activities in New York.

Prevention of Blindness

Proper care of the child begins long before birth. The first acute danger the babe encounters after greeting the world strikes at its vision. Ophthalmia of the new born the doctors call it. It is not inappropriate, therefore, that the exhibit dealing with the prevention of blindness in infants and little children should be at the outposts of the Health section.

Of the 89,000 blind persons in the United States at least one in every four labors through life *in the dark* because the ignorance or carelessness of those who attended him the first hour failed to apply a simple, cheap and harmless remedy before the infection of his eyes could begin. The last census showed more than 4,000 blind in Illinois, though only sixty-four children are under instruction in Chicago schools.

Of the thirty-two little ones in the kindergarten of our state school for the blind at Jacksonville, no less than sixteen, or *fifty per cent,* were sightless because of neglect at their birth. Of new pupils admitted to the schools in as many states in 1907, more than twenty-eight per cent were blind from the same cause. And the remedy is so simple: thorough cleaning of the eyes at birth and the dropping into each of two drops of a one per cent solution of nitrate of silver to neutralize infection. Because it is so simple and quite harmless, every careful physician uses this precaution now. Should he neglect it, however, it is the patient's duty to insist upon it and not take the chance which may put so terrible a handicap upon the babe.

Other causes of blindness and weak vision are pictured on the remaining panels of this sub-section—as well as the measures which are taken to prevent or correct them in many cases but which should be extended to all. How backward girls and boys are transformed from dullards into bright and active youngsters by treatment of their eyes and the fitting of proper glasses; what leads to injuries and defects of vision; what steps are being taken to safeguard the sight of children in and out of the public schools; how children hopelessly blind are saved from dependence and trained to business and professional careers—these and many more vital facts are urged on parents. The need of action is pressing. Of a round 20,000,000 of children of school age in the United States, it is estimated that 8,000 are hampered in their school work by some defect in seeing.

The "Baby Tent"

Infant welfare in the home comes next. Right from the firing line of the "river wards" has been brought a typical "Baby Tent," the emergency hospital and relief station in which the summer ailments of small folk are treated and anxious mothers taught how to restore their little ones to health. Set on flat roofs or vacant lots in districts where a light, clean, airy room suitable for the work could hardly be had for love or money, the Baby Tents have proved a happy solution of the difficult problem of carrying help to the neighborhoods where help was most bitterly needed.

To find these places, consult the last mortality map issued by the Health Department. Dots represent the deaths of infants from diarrhœal diseases. The dots are thickest in the quarters where the three-room house and the house sub-let to several families are most frequent, where the streets are cleaned seldom or not at all, where the poorest milk is sold, the stalest bread, the oldest meat. To combat these forces, which conspire to kill and are hardly less cruel when they spare, the first Baby tack [strategy] on these plague spots of the health chart [was] organized. Ten tents were in operation last summer; 1,753 babies were cared for behind the screened walls of the canvas hospitals and 3,500 more were hunted out for treatment in their homes.

On arrival at the tent, the baby is first taken to the dispensary where the physician on duty examines him, the nurse remaining for consultation. Then the child is removed to the tent, and given a bath and a colonic flushing [enema]. If the clothing is dirty, clean garments are provided.

When the infant is claimed by the mother at five thirty, she receives also the food for the night. If some child in particular need fails to come back, a nurse is sent to investigate. She reports conditions, and if she thinks it advisable, some member of the family is sent to the Baby Tent for the child's food. The milk is sold to those able to pay for it. Much is also given away.

Three in every five of the children cared for are "returned" babies. One in every twenty must be kept all summer. Though the tents have no provision for keeping children over night, in emergency cases this has been done several times, and has resulted in saving lives otherwise lost.

The most important work done in the Baby Tents, perhaps, is the education of the mother. She brings the baby apprehensively. Often she cannot speak English and baby's older brother or sister must come along as interpreter. It takes some coaxing to persuade her to leave the baby, while the treatment often alarms her.

Once converted to the methods of the Baby Tent, a mother becomes an enthusiastic supporter. She brings her neighbors who have ailing babies. They follow the doctor's instructions at home. Whenever possible, a nurse pays a visit, so the good work of the tents is extended to 3,500 babies who have never come into them.

Results were immediate and emphatic. "During the month of August," the bulletin of the Health Department for Sept. 10, 1910, declared, "deaths of babies from diarrhœal disease decreased ten per cent in the congested areas of the city. In the better residence sections of the city, they increased forty-four per cent." The contrast is the best testimony to the effectiveness of the tents as infant relief stations and centers of instruction in common sense care.

Infant Welfare Station

If the baby is to have his "rights"—present comfort and a positive chance of health and strength as he grows up—his parents, and his mother particularly, must learn how to get them for him. In the "Baby Tent" just reviewed, one method of instructing her and bringing relief to the little sufferer was indicated. The glass-walled Infant Welfare Station which adjoins is another hospital-school of infant care which offers help and advice all the year round. One of its functions at the Exhibit is to examine and suggest the proper treatment for any ailing babe that may be presented, as well as to illustrate and demonstrate for observers the best methods of housing, tending, feeding, dressing and safeguarding an infant from disease.

There are ten of these Welfare Stations in the city. Up to the present year the work was carried on only during the summer. In January last it was put on a permanent continuous basis, with a medical director, seven physicians and six nurses. Conferences are held several times a week at each station at established hours and a thorough examination is made of each baby presented. The children are weighed; if there is any falling off or failure to gain the proper amount, the cause is ascertained—sometimes by lengthy questioning of the mother—or the ailment diagnosed and the remedy prescribed.

Frequently the mother volunteers the necessary information; especially if she has been a regular attendant and has learned some of the basic rules of infant health.

"I know why she's lost," one matron explained when the scales registered four ounces less than the week before. "I've been housecleaning and didn't want to be bothered. So whenever she cried, I nursed her and now I see I was wrong. But she'll gain all right next week, doctor, for I'll feed her regular, as you ordered."

This woman had mastered one of the primary rules of baby health. Here are some of them as taught by the Infant Welfare Stations and, indeed, by the city Health Department, the Visiting Nurses, the children's dispensaries and all the other agencies enlisted in the child-saving campaign.

NURSING

Nothing will do the baby so much good as to nurse him. The breast-fed child has two chances for robust health to the "bottle" baby's one. Remember, however, that the mother's condition of mind and body will affect the child. Worry, anger, illness or overwork on the mother's part are as harmful as improper food or lack of cleanliness.

AMOUNT OF FOOD

Feed the baby as often, but only as often, as the doctor directs. More children are overfed than underfed. Most of them are given too much to eat and too little to drink. If baby cries between feeding times, he is probably thirsty. Give him boiled water that has been cooled, but not exposed to the air.

BOTTLE FEEDING

If artificial food must be used, it should be *pure* milk diluted according to the formula. This will vary according to the baby's needs, but the modifying can be done at home. However, it *must* be done under professional direction. Keep the milk on ice or in cold water. Boil all bottles and nipples every day. Use a fresh bottle for each feeding. When the child is old enough to have other food (nine months to one year), prepare the food according to the directions of your physician or the directions given at the welfare station.

SLEEP

A baby should sleep twenty hours of the twenty-four the first month, and from twelve to fifteen hours during the first two years. Daily naps should be taken until he is old enough to go to school. Train the child from birth to sleep from 6 or 7 o'clock at night to 5 or 6 o'clock in the morning. If he is wakeful or sleeps fitfully, it may be because the air in the room is not fresh. Keep the windows open all the time for the sake both of the baby's lungs and nerves.

BATHING

Give the baby a tub bath every day. Wash his eyes and ears very carefully, but *not* his mouth.

CLOTHING

Clothing should be loose, light, warm and washable. Tight bands are bad for the muscles and starch scratches the delicate skin. Don't swaddle him, give him room.

"Have the baby vaccinated when a few months old. Give no medicine except when the doctor prescribes. The effect of 'soothing syrups' is like hitting the child on the head with a hammer.

"If the baby has diarrhœa, give no food, only boiled water, and send for your doctor, or bring him to the welfare station.

"The common house fly is the enemy of health and the chief cause of the deadly summer diaorrhœa. Keep your doors and windows screened, therefore, and keep the flies away from the screens. They will not come where they find no food and they like nothing so well as filth. Milk into which a fly has fallen should be thrown away.

"Do not pick up your baby every time he cries. Teach him for his own sake, as well as yours, to be content alone. Make holding him a treat, not a practice. Keep him quiet; a baby who is 'jiggled' will be a 'nervous' child.

"The baby should be weighed every week, especially if he is bottle-fed. The baby's weight, not his age, determines what modification of milk is necessary."

These and other basic rules of infant care are the subjects of ten-minute talks on "How to Keep the Baby Well," which are given four times daily in the Welfare Station, at 11 in the morning, 4 in the afternoon, and 8 and 9 in the evening. The demonstrations will be by the St. Elizabeth's Day Nursery staff on Fridays, by Henry Booth House on Mondays, Wednesdays and Saturdays, by Davis Square on Sunday, and Chicago Commons, Tuesdays.

More Infant Welfare stations are needed. Twenty nurses would not be too many to carry on the work, and a hospital of one hundred beds devoted exclusively to children under two years would never lack patients. . . .

Mouth Hygiene

Of what use are pure food laws if the food is put into a dirty mouth? This is the question proposed and answered in the dental hygiene room.

Medical science has concluded that the mouth is the chief lodging place of the germs of at least six most dangerous diseases—tuberculosis, diphtheria, scarlet fever, measles, pneumonia and whooping cough. Mouth hygiene, then, is of primary importance. Good health waits on good digestion and good digestion upon good teeth. The care of the teeth should begin before they appear, for in the jaws of the baby are lodged the crowns of his twenty teeth, almost completely formed. The condition in which they come to view depends upon how carefully the baby has been fed before. Most of the difficulties of teething result from indigestion.

There is a harmful notion prevalent that the temporary teeth are of little importance, and that it makes little difference when they are lost. On the contrary, it is of essential importance that they remain in the mouth up to the time the second teeth are ready to take their place. Otherwise the child will probably suffer from feeble digestion brought on by insufficient mastication, or from toothache, a little considered affliction, but one likely to permanently affect the nervous system.

The mother must safeguard the child by careful watching of conditions, and by teaching the child the proper care of the teeth. Cleanliness is the first requirement of health everywhere and pre-eminently of the mouth. This must be supplemented by frequent visits to the dentist to control such disorders as the tooth brush cannot affect.

Children should be taught to brush not only the teeth, but the gums and tongue every morning. This not only cleans them, but stimulates circulation. Brush the upper teeth downward and the lower teeth upward. Pay especial attention to the part of the teeth next [to] the gums. After the brushing the mouth should be thoroughly rinsed with water, taking care that it reaches all the spaces between the teeth.

Supplementing the exhibit will be a dental clinic such as should be in certain public school buildings to look after the care of pupils' teeth. One such clinic is now maintained by the school board and there are four in addition supported by private beneficence. All of these, of course, have established hours for examining the mouths of the children of the neighborhood.

Besides demonstrations of various dental operations there will be short talks—sometimes with live subjects in the chair—on the care of the mouth and teeth.

22

Images from the Chicago Child Welfare Exhibit
1911

Exhibitors told their stories through displays, practical demonstrations, and, overwhelmingly, through the use of posters, which depicted children in distress and children taking part in the many different programs designed for their benefit. The two posters reproduced here reflect the tone projected by many: the gritty photographs showing helpless, hapless children living in dire circumstances; the terse captions; and the thick black lines surrounding each picture that are reminiscent of the mourning bands with which newspaper editors sometimes outlined obituaries and stories about political assassinations and other tragedies.

The official poster of the exhibit, on the other hand, is more optimistic in tone. It draws on the traditional metaphor of Old Man Time turning the world over to the next generation—more familiar to modern readers, perhaps, in commemorating New Year's Day. Note that the hourglass has just been turned over; the "day of the child," to quote Cyrus McCormick, has just begun.

Sophinisba P. Breckinridge, ed., *The Child in the City: A Series of Papers Presented at the Conferences Held during the Chicago Child Welfare Exhibit* (Chicago: Department of Social Investigation, Chicago School of Civics and Philanthropy, 1912).

The Child in the City: A Handbook of the Child Welfare Exhibit at the Coliseum, May 11 to May 25, 1911 (Chicago: Blakely Printing Co., 1911).

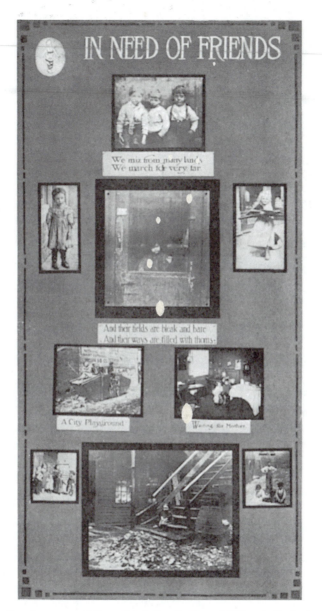

A poster showing some of the grim facts of urban childhood: the lack of recreational facilities, absent parents, hopeless futures.

A poster from the child labor section of the exhibit showing children taking on heavy responsibilities at the expense of their education and talent.

STRENGTHEN THE LITTLE HANDS THAT MUST CARRY ON THE WORLD

The official poster for the Chicago Child Welfare Exhibit, by Lucy Fitch Perkins, the well-known author and illustrator of children's books.

3

The Spirit of Youth

Most observers of city children at the turn of the century wrote about children from an adult's perspective rather than from the children's unique vantage points. Although social scientists did, of course, talk to the children they were researching—the leisure time surveys, for instance, provide wonderful hints of children's voices—the public discussion of child-related issues generally ignored the opinions of children and youth. The following selections offer several types of documents reflecting the points of view of children and youth during the first three decades of the twentieth century. Although each document is unique, this chorus of children's voices reveals the themes of childhood and child welfare in the Progressive Era: the prevalence of class in determining attitudes and experiences, reformers' concern with the moral development of children, and the vibrant cultures of children and youth that developed during this period.

THE NEWSBOYS' WORLD

Newsboys were often viewed as troublemakers and "street arabs" by reformers during the decades before they and other street traders were regulated by state child labor laws in the 1910s. Some state laws established newsboys' republics, self-governing organizations that promoted self-regulation. Milwaukee's was one of the most active and long-lived. In addition to forming political parties, holding annual elections, enforcing various elements of the street trades (e.g., newsboys were supposed to wear badges proving they had a work permit and could only work during certain hours), and organizing sports and social activities, the Milwaukee Republic also published *The Newsboys' World* between 1916 and 1934. Written and edited by the newsboys themselves, each issue cost a nickel and featured news stories, editorials, and letters to the editor on issues important to the several thousand young men who sold newspapers in Milwaukee.

The following articles reflect the newsboys' enthusiasm for the political and economic systems of the United States and their confidence that their work as newsboys would help them get ahead.

23

THE NEWSBOYS' WORLD

Stick!

March 1916

Child welfare reformers sought to bring order to the lives of children and youth, who needed to be taught the virtues of hard work, perseverance, and ambition. There is no doubt that the young author of this editorial, himself a newsboy, agreed with reformers about the necessary ingredients to success in business and in life.

If you are ambitious and expect to win any battles in life you must learn one thing and that is to Stick! Stick! Stick!

Often do boys, without great ideals, lose out in the game of life because they have not learned to stick. They no sooner tackle a thing and find some difficulty, than they give up all hope and drop out. They not only lose out but they also disgrace themselves and people lose all respect for them because they lack will power and a strong personality.

You will strike many things in your life which are very hard to accomplish. You will come across people in organizations who will disgust you. But don't give up because of that. Stick to your job no matter what the circumstances are and at the end you will become the master of the situation.

24

THE NEWSBOYS' WORLD

Lest We Forget

January 1921

Milwaukee newsboys eagerly participated in the Newsboys' Republic and generally accepted the rules under which it operated. But they still had to be reminded from time to time of what they could not do and what it meant to wear a street trader's badge. The rules listed in this editorial include not only regulations established by the state child labor laws, but also standards of behavior established by the republic. These rules were a response to critics of street trading by children, who had long complained, among other things, of children working late into the night and gambling and smoking during their off hours.

Are you living up to the rules which you promised to obey when you received your street trades badge? For the purpose of reminding you of their importance, we are inserting them in this issue. Check them over with your own record and in case you have fallen down on any particular rule—NOW is a splendid chance to brace up.

I WILL attend school regularly.

I WILL strive to bring my SCHOLARSHIP and DEPORTMENT to the highest possible standard.

I WILL always wear my badge over my heart in **plain sight** while engaged in any street trade.

I WILL carry my permit with me and be ready to show the same when directed.

I WILL return my badge to the Supervisor of Street Trades, when I reach the age of seventeen, give up the newspaper work, or leave school.

I WILL always keep my accounts straight with the newspaper men with whom I deal.

I WILL be courteous at all times.

I WILL NOT sell or deliver during school hours.

The Newsboys' World, Jan. 1921.

I WILL NOT sell before 5:00 A.M., or after 7:30 P.M.

I WILL NOT allow any boy to help me who does not own a legal Street Trades badge and permit.

I WILL NOT let any other boy use my badge and permit.

I WILL NOT shine shoes or carry hand baggage without a special permit.

I WILL NOT STEAL.

I WILL NOT GAMBLE in any form.

I WILL abstain from using tobacco in any form, will refrain from swearing, to the best of my ability.

When granted my badge by the Supervisor of Street Trades, I promise to live up to the Laws of Wisconsin and of the Newsboys' Republic, and to do everything in my power to become a **useful newsboy** in the City of Milwaukee.

25

THE NEWSBOYS' WORLD

What Is Required of the Ideal Successful Newsboy?

April 1927

The Newsboys' World *sponsored periodic contests inviting newsboys of all ages to describe proper conduct and the best ways to sell newspapers. These winning essays from a 1927 contest describe the "ideal" newsboy as a good businessman, but also as a useful member of the community.*

Sixth Grade Division Prize Essay

BY CARL NISENKORN

We want Milwaukee newsboys to be the best in Wisconsin. In order to do this every newsboy should be loyal, honest and respectful. He must not steal and swear. He must be polite at all times, and respect the rules he is taught before he can become a newsboy. When a boy makes promises he should keep them, for his own good, as well as for the good of the community in which he lives.

Loyalty does not only mean loyalty to your country but to everybody. A newsboy must be loyal to his city, state and town, to his school, his friends and his home.

It is necessary for a newsboy to be honest. He cannot get on with his paper dealers if he is dishonest. He must pay his bills on time. He must be honest not only in his professions but in all his dealings.

Newsboys in order to be successful must be polite. When making a sale it is well to say "Thank you." The average boy finds that he profits by this at very little expense. The boy who is loyal, honest and courteous in boyhood will be most successful in manhood.

Eighth Grade Division

BY ROBERT PENTLER

An ideal newsboy should have, we think, certain clearly defined qualities. First of all he should be a boy of unquestionable character. He should be absolutely honest in all things; he should be polite, energetic and alert, ready at all times to do his share of work in the class room and in his contact with the public. He must be a boy who respects his parents, his teachers and the rights of his schoolmates. These qualities will assure popularity and these an Ideal Newsboy must possess. His motto is, "Service and Not Self."

Salesmanship. But an Ideal Newsboy must be something more than a fine fellow. He must possess that subtle something called salesmanship; that quality which induces the public to buy his wares. This quality is a touch of genius. One must be born with it and one must study to develop it. Every day the Ideal Newsboy will say to himself, "How can I become a better salesman?" To do this he must be wide-awake at all times to the possibilities of improvement, and he must always study how to become ever more courteous and gentlemanlike to his customers. From salesmen or salesboys only will people be glad to patronize. The ideals set forth in the Golden Rule are nowhere more applicable than in the case of a genuine 100% newsboy. Let's all do as we would be done by, and success is certain.

High School Division Prize Essay

BY EDWARD POPLAWSKI

The typical American boy is found among the newsboys. A newsboy has certain other duties to perform besides delivering his newspapers. He must strive to increase his business instead of decreasing it. He ought to have the honesty, politeness and courtesy of any Boy Scout and the kindness of a mother.

He can keep his business going up by canvassing a few homes a day and trying to get some of the non-subscribers in his territory to take the newspaper that he is delivering. He can keep his business from decreasing by giving the best service he can to his customers.

He should never charge his customers more than he ought to for the paper. He should never talk back to his customers when they complain about the service they get from him.

A newsboy ought to help small children in crossing the streets whenever an opportunity comes. His kindness can be shown by the way he treats his fellow newsies.

DELINQUENT CHILDHOODS

Clifford R. Shaw was a faculty member at the University of Chicago and part of the famed Chicago school of sociology. Along with other sociologists investigating juvenile delinquency in the 1920s and 1930s, Shaw believed that environmental conditions and the breakdown of community institutions were to blame for the high rate of juvenile delinquency in urban ghettos. His "social disorganization" theory argued that rapid industrialization, the instability of new immigrant communities, and other conditions inherent in urban life caused stresses that young boys "naturally" reacted to by rebelling and engaging in criminal behavior.

The following documents, although excerpted from books written or compiled from the points of view of adults, offer slices of life from the vantage points of the young people themselves.

26

VICE COMMISSION OF THE CITY OF CHICAGO

Tantine's Story

1911

"Tantine's Story" is recorded in the Chicago Vice Commission's 1911 study of prostitution, The Social Evil in Chicago: Study of Existing Conditions with Recommendations. *Progressive researchers typically included case studies and personal testimony to give a human dimension to their statistics. While Tantine's story exemplifies how loose morals and a lack of family support could set a young girl on a downward spiral to prostitution, it also allows glimpses of Tantine's personality, revealing a spunky, independent-minded young woman who apparently did not share the middle-class values of the reformers who mourned her lost innocence. Researchers replaced specific names and addresses with coded references — (X958), for instance — in order to protect the anonymity of their sources.*

Tantine (X952). About 19 years of age. Is a blonde. Has been a prostitute for three years. Been soliciting in (X953) for six months. She lives at (X954) Wabash avenue. Flat (X955). Quite a number of prostitutes live in this flat. She pays four dollars per week for room and bath.

Tantine's parents live in (X956). She went home last summer, and told her parents she was married and had a "rich husband."

When she was 16 years of age she met a man named (X957), who promised to marry her, and on the strength of this promise seduced her.

They then planned to elope. He took her to (X958), Wyoming, and put her in a sporting house.

The following is given in practically her own words:

"I was a little mutt, then, and I did not know where I was. The landlady just asked my name and how old I was. I told her 16. She

---

Vice Commission of the City of Chicago, *The Social Evil in Chicago: Study of Existing Conditions with Recommendations* (Chicago: Vice Commission of the City of Chicago, 1911), 196–98.

said I looked it. You bet I did. I wore my hair in a braid, and it was parted in the center flat on my head. I also wore short skirts. It was a pretty house, and the madame told me to stay up in my room. She asked how I came to know (X957), and I told her he was my husband. I did not see him again until late that night. In a short while the landlady called me down from my room and introduced me to an elderly gentleman, and told me to go up to my room with him. I told her I did not want to go up to my room with any one but my husband. She said that man was going to give me a whole lot of money, if I just went up to my room with him. I finally decided to go up with him. He asked me if I wanted some wine. I told him no. Then the landlady called me aside and said 'Order it anyway, and if you can't drink it, why ditch it.' When we got up to my room, I said, 'Yes, I'll have some wine, and ditch it.' He started to laugh, and called the landlady up and told her what I had said. The landlady laughed and said, 'She is only a little rum, don't mind her.' He then explained to me that ditch it meant to throw it away, when he was not looking.

After talking for a short while, he said it was about time that he made me work. I asked what he meant, and he said, 'Take your clothes off, and I'll show you.' I felt highly insulted and told him so. He then told me where I was, and what I was up against, and I started to cry. He then gave me $50 and told me to go home to my mother, cause he said that was where I belonged.

I did not see anybody else that day, and late that night (X957) came back and told me that he already was married and he had a child. He said that he was going to (X961) to get a divorce and then marry me. At the same time he took the $50 away from me.

I was only here one day, because the next day I met a fellow who was going to (X962), and he asked me to go along. I consented and went with him. I lived with him for nearly a year. He was the second fellow I ever stayed with. (X957) actually violated me. He forced me, and I was going to tell my mother only he promised to marry me. No, I did not like him so very much.

While in (X964) city, I had a quarrel with my fellow, and left him. I took the train for (X965), because I had heard so much about it. I "hustled" there for about a week, when I met (X966), a very prominent doctor of (X965). He was a married man, and he put me up in a swell hotel and gave me all the money I needed; he only came to see me about three times a week. All went well for about a month until one day I was arrested by the chief of police himself. He took me into his office, and showed me a picture of myself which my father and mother had sent him in order to locate me. I denied that I was Tantine and said I did not have any parents and that I came from (X968). He then asked me to name a few of the principal streets of (X968) and I was stuck. I told him I could not remember them now, as I was not there very long, as I spent most of my life in (X968). He asked me about (X968), and I got away with that all right. I then told him that that picture could not be of me as I was much older. I did age fearfully after that. I look much older than 19, don't I? He talked to me for about two hours, and I bulled him, and he finally let me go.

Everything was all right until one day I ran into a fellow from home who also knew (X966). He promised to take me to Chicago and I decided to go with him. He then wrote to (X973), who was in (X974) at the time with his wife and child. When we arrived in Chicago my friend put me in (X975) house, (X976) Dearborn street. About a week later (X957) and his wife came to Chicago. He came up to see me and wanted me to live with him. I bawled him out and threatened to turn him over to the police or kill him, if I ever saw him again. That same day his wife came over to see me and she told me that he did the same thing to her. He seduced her and when she had a baby her folks made him marry her. She said he was leading her and the child a dog's life, but she stuck for the child's sake. He was the prettiest baby I ever saw. I believe they are living in (X978) now.

I left (X975) house in about two months, and have been in a lot of houses. I have been in places where they graft, almost hold you up. I have hustled on the street. Yes, I used to pay lots of protection money to policemen. But I got wise in time. If they threaten to pinch me, why I say, go ahead and pinch me, then they won't. No, you can't make any money hustling on the street any more. If you want to be in right you have got to give half of what you make to the coppers. No, I never knew any of their names, but I could point them out to you any time. Hell, they all graft. There is not a policeman around here that doesn't hold us girls up, and I know it from experience. But you see us girls who have been around a long time get wise, and they don't get a nickel out of me any more.

I go home at 3:00 a.m. every morning, and I don't hustle any place any more but here. I think I make more than any of the girls around here, and I don't spend it on booze like the rest of them. That's why they never have anything. I make on an average of $100 a week. That's pretty good, isn't it. Well, come up to the house some afternoon, and see me. No, I don't live with anybody. It don't pay."

27

CLIFFORD R. SHAW

The Jack-Roller: A Delinquent Boy's Own Story
1930

The Jack-Roller *is a unique account of a delinquent named Stanley, who grew up in Chicago's "Back of the Yards" neighborhood, a heavily Irish and Polish area near the stockyards. Part sociological treatise and part memoir by a reformed delinquent,* The Jack-Roller *(a "jack" was the target of robberies, or "rolling") is a chilling portrayal of a young life gone horribly awry. The excerpts below are Stanley's description of his early life and a partial list of his many encounters with the police, the court system, and correctional institutions before the age of eighteen.*

Starting Down Grade

As far back as I can remember, my life was filled with sorrow and misery. The cause was my stepmother, who nagged me, beat me, insulted me, and drove me out of my own home. My mother died when I was four years old, so I never knew a real mother's affection. My father remarried when I was five years of age. The stepmother who was to take the place of my real mother was a rawboned woman, devoid of features as well as emotions. She was of Polish stock, and had the habits and customs of the people of the Old World. She came to America when about thirty years old; was married at the time, and had seven children. Her husband was in ill health and he died soon after arriving in Chicago. After burying her husband, she found herself without financial resources for herself and children. Realizing her predicament and the necessity of immediate action, she ventured out to find a husband, a man to support herself and her seven children; literally to slave and labor and bring home the bacon. Her venture was not so successful at first. Men were not wont to fall for her precious

---

Clifford R. Shaw, *The Jack-Roller: A Delinquent Boy's Own Story* (Chicago: University of Chicago Press, 1930), 47–52, 25–29.

few charms. And, besides, did she not have seven children as an
added burden?

My father was in a similar predicament, my mother having died and
left three children. His thoughts went in quest of a woman to be his
wife and a mother to his children. So it happened that Fate brought
about a meeting of the two. A hasty courtship ensued, and in a short
time they were married. My father worked for the Gas Company, and
my stepmother proceeded to establish a home.

To this day I wonder how my father could have picked out such a
woman for a wife. My conclusion is that she, in her desperation, used
all her charm and coercion to get a man — any man who was able and
inclined to work. My father, being fond of his whiskey and beer,
and being in need of a mistress, became intoxicated and, thus blinded
to her nature and circumstances, yielded to her coercion.

She brought her seven children to our home. With us three children, my brother, my sister, and myself, there were twelve to feed and
clothe. We all lived in four rooms in a basement. My father did not
whimper. All he asked for was his regular meals, a bed to sleep in, and
his daily can of beer and whisky. His mind was like a motor, always on
one course. He didn't think of his children as boys and girls to be
loved. He thought of us as just "kids," who had to be provided for, and
he was the good provider. There his parental duties ended. Never did
he show any love or kindness. We "kids" were worth boarding and tol-
erating because sometime we would be financial assets.

For six months things went rather smoothly. Then my troubles began. My father and stepmother began to argue and quarrel about us
children. I didn't know much about it at first, for I was more interested
in playing with the cat behind the stove. But I soon felt the change.
From a quiet woman, the stepmother changed to a hell-cat full of
venom and spite. The first time she struck me was when I was in my
favorite nook behind the stove, playing with the cat. She pulled me out
and beat me, striking me in the face and on the back with her hard
and bony hand. That was the first time that I ever knew fear. After
many beatings I became more and more afraid, and I crouched behind
the stove in fear. Well do I remember my first fears and horrors of
her. I became unhappy and did not caper and play with my brother
and sister as I had been wont to do. My father gave me no comfort.
He spent his time at work, at the saloon, and in bed. Never did he pet
or cheer me.

The stepmother favored her own children in every way. They
received what luxuries were to be had, while my brother and sister

and I had crumbs to pick off the table. She let her children eat at the table, and made us wait. Whenever one of her children would do a wrong they would tell her that I did it, and then I, instead of the culprit, would get the beating. My father couldn't interfere, because if he did the stepmother would threaten to leave. That would have been the best thing for his children, but of course he didn't want her to go.

Things went on this way. We fought with her because she favored her children at meals and beat us for their misdemeanors. Hard indeed it was for me to get enough to eat. Often when I would go to the store to buy food for the family, I would take a little biscuit or anything I could without my stepmother knowing it. So that much was I ahead when I got my portion at mealtime. My father worked steady and received good wages, so there was no good reason why we could not have enough to eat. But the stepmother was saving and fed her own children and let us go starved and half-naked on the street.

The stepmother also made us (brother, sister, and myself) do all the hard work in the house. And then she would beat us if we complained. That is what embittered me against her and her children. I developed a hatred against her that still lasts; a hatred that was so burning that when she would look into my eyes she would read it there, and in that way she knew my feeling. The Lord knows I tried to love her, but my nature could not stand her caresses in one of those sympathetic moods which she seldom had. Occasionally she would seem to feel sorry for her abuses and cruelty, and would ask me to kiss her; but my feelings protested. My fear and hatred made me avoid her and resent her caresses. Then she would get angry and beat me.

So I grew old enough to go out on the street. The life in the streets and alleys became fascinating and enticing. I had two close companions that I looked up to with childish admiration and awe. One was William, my stepbrother. The other one was Tony, a dear friend of my stepbrother, William. They were close friends, four years older than me and well versed in the art of stealing.

To my child-seeing eyes, I visioned Tony as a great leader in the neighborhood, and he directed his gang around with much bravado. He and William were always stealing and talking about stealing and I fell in with them as soon as I began to play around in the neighborhood.

Tony was a squatty boy, rough features, closely set eyes, and a body that bespoke strength and ruggedness. With his strength and fighting ability, he maintained leadership over his gang. He was also daring and courageous. I remember vividly how awed I was by his daring in stealing and fighting. These things made him a guy to be looked up to and respected in the neighborhood.

Tony liked his whiskey and in our neighborhood one could find as many as four or five saloons in one block in those days. He would dare me to drink and I would, although it burned my throat. I was what they call "game" and I just swallowed it without a word, to maintain that high distinction which I was openly proud of.

Tony had two sisters who always played with us and went on our stealing adventures. They could steal as good as any boy. Also they had sex relations openly with all the boys in the neighborhood. I remember how the boys boasted that they had had sex relations with each of them. All the boys talked about it and the girls didn't care; they seemed to be proud of it and expect it. The funny thing about it was that Tony knew all about his sisters and their behavior and only made merry about it.

The boys in the gang teased me about Tony's sisters, asking me how many times I had had sex relations with them. Even the girls would talk to me about sex things, put their arms around me, and touch my body. At first I was too young to know what it all meant, but I soon learned and developed many sex habits, like masturbation and playing with girls.

Tony didn't work, but made his money by stealing, and he made lots of it for a boy of his age.

My stepmother sent me out with William (my stepbrother) to pick rags and bottles in the alleys. She said that would pay for my board and make me more useful than fretting and sulking at home. I did not mind that in the least. In fact, I enjoyed it, because I was at least out of the old lady's reach. I began to have a great time exploring the whole neighborhood—romping and playing in the alleys and "prairies," gathering rags, bones, and iron, and selling them to the rag peddlers. This romping and roaming became fascinating and appealed to my curiosity, because it was freedom and adventure. We played "Indian" and other games in the alleys, running through the old sheds and vacant houses. Then we gathered cigarette "buttses" along the street and took them to the shed, where we smoked and planned adventure. I was little and young, but I fell in with the older boys. Outside, in the neighborhood, life was full of pleasure and excitement, but at home it was dull and drab and full of nagging, quarreling, and beating, and stuffy and crowded besides. . . .

Official Record of Arrests and Commitments

This section includes the official account of Stanley's arrests and commitments, which was compiled from the records of the police, juvenile court, correctional institutions, social agencies, and behavior clinics. This record shows clearly the sequence of behavior problems, proceeding from the minor difficulties of truancy and petty stealing, at the early age of six years, to the more serious delinquency of "jack-rolling" and burglary, in the adolescent period.

1. Six years, six months of age:
   Found sleeping under a doorstep late at night several blocks away from his home. He was in the company of an older boy, and had been away from home two days. Returned to his home by the police.
2. Six years, six months:
   Picked up by the police as a runaway and released to the father. Boy was in the company of the same companion, and had been away from home three days.
3. Six years, seven months:
   Picked up as a lost boy and placed in the police station. Parents were notified and the boy was released to them. Had been away four days.
4. Six years, seven months:
   Picked up by the police and placed in the Detention Home. Released to parents. Had been away from home one week.
5. Six years, nine months:
   Found sleeping in an alley four blocks away from his home. Had been away from home five days. Was in the company of an older companion. Complained that his stepmother beat him. Placed in Detention Home and later released to the father.
6. Six years, nine months:
   Picked up as a runaway and placed in the Juvenile Detention Home. Held one day and released to the father.
7. Six years, eleven months:
   Police found the boy begging food at a bakery near Halsted and Madison Streets, four miles away from home. He had been away three weeks. Told police he "didn't like it at home." Said stepmother beat him up. Released to father at police station. . . .

After being enrolled in school, the boy was released to the father under supervision of the probation officer.

19. Eight years, eleven months:
    Arrested on a charge of truancy and stealing from railroads.

Had been away from home and school two weeks. Placed in Detention Home. Released two weeks later to live at home.

20. Nine years, one month:

Arrested and brought to court. Boy told the court: "Do not want to live at home. Stepmother hollers on me and beats me. I want to live with the Irish woman and her kids." Boy released to live at home pending investigation of the home of the Irish lady, where he was living at time of arrest. Ran away from home same day.

21. Nine years, one month:

Voluntarily went to the Detention Home to seek shelter, having been away from home one week.

22. Nine years, one month:

Committed to Chicago Parental School.

23. Nine years, seven months:

Paroled from the Chicago Parental School to live at home.

24. Nine years, seven months:

Found sleeping in an alley near Halsted and Madison streets. Had been away from home four days. Released to father at police station.

25. Nine years, eight months:

Picked up by police as a runaway. Placed in Detention Home and later brought to court. In court the officer stated: "This boy has been before the court many times for absenting himself from home without cause. He ran away about two weeks ago. Stepmother asks that he be committed to an institution." In responding to the court, the boy stated: "I want to live in the Detention Home and never go back home." Placed on probation to live at home.

26. Nine years, nine months:

Arrested and brought to court charged with truancy and stealing. Was with another boy. It was stated in court that "this boy is an habitual runaway. He has been given many opportunities at home but does not appreciate them." Committed to the St. Charles School for Boys.

27. Eleven years:

Paroled from St. Charles to live at home.

28. Eleven years, one month:

Picked up by police at Desplaines and Madison streets (six miles from home). He was eating stolen buns and garbage in the alley when the officer found him. Boy said parents were dead. Taken to the Detention Home, where he was identified and sent home.

29. Eleven years, one month:

Went to Hull-House Social Settlement seeking food and shelter.

Placed in the hands of the police and returned to the St. Charles School for boys.

30. Eleven years, eleven months:
Paroled to live in a farm near Batavia, Illinois.

31. Twelve years, two months:
Ran away from farm.

32. Twelve years, two months:
Arrested on West Madison Street as a vagrant. Placed in Detention Home and later paroled to father.

33. Twelve years, seven months:
Arrested in the Y.M.C.A. Hotel. Had been away from home five months. Placed in Detention Home and returned to St. Charles.

34. Fourteen years:
Paroled to stepmother.

35. Fifteen years:
Arrested on West Madison Street, charged with burglary and "jack-rolling." Had been away from home eight months. Placed in the county jail. Case came up in the Boy's Court, and boy committed to the Illinois State Reformatory at Pontiac for a definite term of one year.

36. Sixteen years, one month:
Released from the Reformatory.

37. Sixteen years, nine months:
Arrested on West Madison Street, charged with burglary and "jack-rolling." Had been away from home seven months. Placed in the county jail and a few days later committed to the Chicago House of Correction for a definite sentence of one year.

38. Seventeen years, eight months:
Released from the House of Correction.

REMEMBERED CHILDHOODS

Memoirs and autobiographies are staples of historical research, but they must be used carefully. The human tendency to justify one's actions, to romanticize the past (Harpo Marx's memoir tends in that direction), and to forget details about long ago events are all factors to consider when interpreting memoirs and autobiographies. The three memoirs excerpted below are straightforward accounts of hardscrabble childhoods: one by an immigrant and two by African Americans who would overcome their humble beginnings to become world famous as a politician, a performer, and a poet, respectively.

28

GOLDA MEIR

My Life

1975

Golda Mabovitz (1898–1978), who as Golda Meir would serve as prime minister of Israel from 1969 to 1974, came to the United States from Russia in 1906 with her mother, and her sisters Sheyna and Zipke. Her father had come three years earlier, settling in Milwaukee. Meir's memoir records the difficulties faced by most immigrant families as they tried to assimilate into American life while at the same time retaining at least some of their religious and cultural traditions. But it is also the story of a young girl's fascination with her adopted city and of the ways that she took advantage of the vibrant ethnic and political culture in which she lived. Although her parents were not at first in favor of her continuing her education, she did go to high school and graduate. She also attended Milwaukee Normal School (a teachers' training college), and married. By the early 1920s, Meir and her husband were in Palestine working for the formation of a Jewish state.

My father met us in Milwaukee, and he seemed changed: beardless, American-looking, in fact a stranger. He hadn't managed to find an apartment for us yet, so we moved, temporarily and not comfortably, into his one room in a house that belonged to a family of recently arrived Polish Jews. Milwaukee—even the small part of it that I saw during those first few days—overwhelmed me: new food, the baffling sounds of an entirely unfamiliar language, the confusion of getting used to a parent I had almost forgotten. It all gave me a feeling of unreality so strong that I can still remember standing in the street and wondering who and where I was.

I suppose that being together with his family again after so long was not easy for my father either. At any rate, even before we really had time to rest up from the journey or get to know him again, he did a most extraordinary thing: Refusing to listen to any arguments,

---

Golda Meir, *My Life* (New York: Dell, 1975), 28–32, 35–37.

on the morning after our arrival he determinedly marched all of us downtown on a shopping expedition. He was horrified, he said, by our appearance. We looked so dowdy and "Old World," particularly Sheyna in her matronly black dress. He insisted on buying us all new clothes, as though by dressing us differently he could turn us, within twenty-four hours, into three American-looking girls. His first purchase was for Sheyna—a frilly blouse and a straw hat with a broad brim covered in poppies, daisies and cornflowers. "Now you look like a human being," he said. "This is how we dress in America." Sheyna immediately burst into tears of rage and shame. "Maybe that's how you dress in America," she shouted, "but I am certainly not going to dress like that!" She absolutely refused to wear either the hat or the blouse, and I think perhaps that premature excursion downtown marked the actual start of what were to be years of tension between them.

Not only were their personalities very different, but for three long years Father had been receiving complaining letters from Mother about Sheyna and her selfish behavior, and in his heart of hearts he must have blamed Sheyna for his not having been able to go back to Russia again and the family's having to come to the States. Not that he was unhappy in Milwaukee. On the contrary, by the time we came he was already part of the immigrant life there. He was a member of a synagogue, he had joined a trade union (he was employed, off and on, in the workshops of the Milwaukee railroad), and he had accumulated a number of cronies. In his own eyes, he was on the way to becoming a full-fledged American Jew, and he liked it. The last thing in the world he wanted was a disobedient, sullen daughter who demanded the right to live and dress in Milwaukee as though it were Pinsk, and the argument that first morning in Schuster's Department Store was soon to develop into a far more serious conflict. But I was delighted by my pretty new clothes, by the soda pop and ice cream and by the excitement of being in a real skyscraper, the first five-story building I had ever seen. In general, I thought Milwaukee was wonderful. Everything looked so colorful and fresh, as though it had just been created, and I stood for hours staring at the traffic and the people. The automobile in which my father had fetched us from the train was the first I had ever ridden in, and I was fascinated by what seemed like the endless procession of cars, trolleys and shiny bicycles on the street.

We went for a walk, and I peered, unbelieving, into the interior of the drugstore with its papier-mâché fisherman advertising cod-liver oil, the barbershop with its weird chairs and the cigar store with its wooden Indian. I remember enviously watching a little girl of my own age dressed up in her Sunday best, with puffed sleeves and high-button shoes, proudly wheeling a doll that reclined grandly on a pillow of its own, and marveling at the sight of the women in long white skirts and men in white shirts and neck-ties. It was all completely strange and unlike anything I had seen or known before, and I spent the first days in Milwaukee in a kind of trance. . . .

I started school in a huge, fortresslike building on Fourth Street near Milwaukee's famous Schlitz beer factory, and I loved it. I can't remember how long it took me to learn English (at home, of course, we spoke Yiddish, and luckily, so did almost everyone else on Walnut Street), but I have no recollection of the language ever being a real problem for me, so I must have picked it up quickly. I made friends quickly, too. Two of those early first- or second-grade friends remained friends all my life, and both live in Israel now. One was Regina Hamburger (today Medzini), who lived on our street and who was to leave America when I did; the other was Sarah Feder, who became one of the leaders of Labor Zionism in the United States. Anyhow, coming late to class almost every day was awful, and I used to cry all the way to school. Once a policeman even came to the shop to explain to my mother about truancy. She listened attentively but barely understood anything he said, so I went on being late for school and sometimes never got there at all—an ever greater disgrace. My mother—not that she had much alternative—didn't seem to be moved by my bitter resentment of the shop. "We have to live, don't we?" she claimed, and if my father and Sheyna—each for his and her own reasons—would not help, that didn't mean *I* was absolved of the task. "So it will take you a little longer to become a *rebbetzin* [a bluestocking]," she added. I never became a bluestocking [intellectual or literary woman] of course, but I learned a lot at that school. . . .

At all events, apart from the shop and being aware of Sheyna's evident misery about having to live at home—and having had to part from Shamai, who was still in Russia and whom she missed terribly—I think back on those five years in Milwaukee with great pleasure. There was so much to see and do and learn that the memory of Pinsk was almost erased. Almost but not entirely. In September, when we had been in America just over three months, my father told us to be sure and watch the famous Labor Day parade in which he, too, would be marching. Dressed up in our new clothes, Mother, Zipke and I took our places at the street corner he recommended and waited for the parade to begin, not knowing exactly what a parade was, but looking forward to it anyway. Suddenly Zipke saw the mounted police who led the parade. She was absolutely terrified. "It's the Cossacks [Russian soldiers who terrorized Jews]! The Cossacks are coming!" she screamed, and sobbed so hard that she had to be taken home and put to bed. But for me, that parade—the crowds, the brass bands, the floats, the smell of popcorn and hot dogs—symbolized American freedom. Police on horseback were actually escorting the marchers, instead of dispersing them and trampling them underfoot, as they were doing in Russia, and I felt the impact of a new way of life. I didn't know or care about it then—or for some time to come—but it occurs to me now that both Wisconsin in general and Milwaukee in particular were blessed by extremely liberal administrations. Milwaukee was a city of immigrants and had a strong socialist tradition, a socialist mayor for many years and America's first socialist congressman, Victor Berger. But of course, we would have responded in much the same way to any kind of parade in any American city; or maybe there really was some special vitality about Labor Day then, in Milwaukee, a city to which so many German liberals and intellectuals had fled after the unsuccessful Revolution of 1848 and which was as well known for its vigorous trade unions as for its beer gardens. In any case, to see my father marching on that September day was like coming out of the dark into the light. . . .

School absorbed me, and in the little time I had left over from the shop (and helping my mother at home and Zipke—who had now been renamed Clara by Mr. Finn, the school principal—with her lessons) I read and read. Every now and then, Regina Hamburger and I got tickets (perhaps through the school) for a play or a movie. Those were very rare treats, and to this day I remember one of them distinctly—seeing *Uncle Tom's Cabin* and suffering through every moment of it with Uncle Tom and Eva. I can still recall jumping to my feet in the theater, literally beside myself with hatred for Simon Legree. I think it must have been the first thing I ever saw on a stage, and I told my mother and Clara the story over and over again. It had a kind of special reality for all of us.

One important (to me) event took place when I was in the fourth grade. I got involved in my first "public work." Although school in Milwaukee was free, a nominal sum was charged for textbooks, which many of the children in my class could not afford. Obviously, someone had to do something to solve the problem, so I decided to launch a fund. It was to be my very first experience as a fund raiser, but hardly the last!

Regina and I collected a group of girls from the school, explained the purpose of the fund, and we all painted posters announcing that the American Young Sisters Society (we were particularly proud of the name we had made up for our nonexistent organization) was to hold a public meeting on the subject of textbooks. Then, having appointed myself chairman of the society, I hired a hall and sent invitations out to the entire district. Today it seems incredible to me that anyone would agree to rent a hall to a child of eleven but the meeting took place as scheduled one Saturday evening, and dozens of people came. The program was very simple: I spoke about the need for all children to have textbooks whether they had money or not, and Clara, who was then about eight, recited a socialist poem in Yiddish. I can see her now, a very small red-headed child, standing in front of the audience in Packen Hall, gesturing dramatically as she declaimed. The result of the meeting was twofold: A considerable amount of money (by our standards) was raised, and my parents showered praise on Clara and me while walking home that evening. I only wished that Sheyna [hospitalized for tuberculosis] had been there. But at least I could send her the clipping together with a picture of me, from a Milwaukee paper that referred to the meeting:

> A score of little children who give their playtime and scant pennies to charity, and charity organized on their own initiative, too. . . . And it is worthy of comment that this charity is itself a loud comment on the fact that little children may go to the public schools without proper provision of books. Think what that means. . . .

The letter I wrote to Sheyna about the meeting was almost as dramatic as Clara's poem. "Dear Sister," it read, "Now I can tell you that we had the greatest success that there ever was in Packen Hall. And the entertainment was grand. . . ."

My mother had begged me to write out my speech, but it made more sense to me to say what I wanted to say, what was in my heart. And considering it was my first public address, I think I did rather well. At any rate, with the exception of major policy statements at the United Nations or the Knesset, I never got into the habit of using a written text, and I went on for the next half century making "speeches from my head," as I described it to Sheyna in that letter I wrote her in the summer of 1909.

Eventually, during the summer vacation, Regina and I got our first real jobs: very junior salesgirls at a department store downtown. What we really did, for the most part, was wrap packages and run errands; but we made a few dollars each week, and I was released from having to stand in our shop all day. My father, very much against his will, took my place there, and it was with a sense of great independence that I pressed my skirt and blouse each evening and set out at dawn each day to walk to work. It was a long walk, but the carfare I saved went toward a winter coat—the first thing I ever bought with my own earnings.

When I was fourteen, I finished elementary school. My marks were good, and I was chosen to be class valedictorian. The future seemed very bright and clear to me. Obviously I would go on to high school and then, perhaps, even become a teacher, which is what I most wanted to be. I thought—and still think today—that teaching is the noblest and the most satisfying profession of all. A good teacher opens up the whole world for children, makes it possible for them to learn to use their minds and in many ways equips them for life. I *knew* I could teach well, once I was sufficiently educated myself, and I wanted that kind of responsibility. Regina, Sarah and I talked endlessly about what we would do when we grew up. I remember on those summer evenings how we sat for hours on the steps of my house and discussed our futures. Like teenage girls everywhere, we thought these were the most important decisions we would ever have to take— other than marriage, and that certainly seemed much too remote to be worth our talking about.

29

JOSEPHINE BAKER

Josephine

1976

Josephine Baker (1906–1975) was a celebrated and sometimes contro-versial singer and dancer in Europe and around the world. But before she became famous she was a poor little African American girl living in the slums of St. Louis. Her most vivid childhood memory was the terror

---

Josephine Baker and Jo Bouillon, *Josephine,* translated by Mariana Fitzpatrick (New York: Harper & Row, 1976), 6–9, 13–17.

and destruction of the 1917 East St. Louis race riot, which resulted in the deaths of thirty-nine African Americans and nine whites. But the opening chapter of her memoir, published after her death and including the recollections of her sister Margaret, focuses chiefly on the Baker family's day-to-day struggle for survival and Josephine's introduction to show business.

I spent most of my time wandering around the colored quarter. Unlike Aunt Elvara, who detested our neighborhood, I thought it was terribly exciting. Especially on Saturdays. Everyone seemed to own an accordion, a banjo or harmonica. Those without enough money for real instruments made banjos from cheese boxes. We played music that to us was beautiful on everything from clothesline strung across barrel halves to paper-covered combs. As soon as the music began, I would move my arms and legs in all directions in time to the rhythm or mark the beat with my friends on the treasure we pulled from the trash: tin cans, battered saucepans, abandoned wooden and metal containers. What a wonderful time we had! Sometimes lamplight in a window would indicate that a rent party was in progress. The nickels and dimes collected for the refreshments served at these gatherings helped the needy host to pay his rent. I never had a cent of my own, so could only hope to poke my head through the door long enough to catch a glimpse of an ancient piano someone had dragged in, the piano player's round-tipped yellow shoe, a flash of green sock, the sleeve of his pink shirt and the end of his cigarette, which almost touched the hat brim tilted low over one eye. A woman's voice bawled: "Do one little thing, papa, a long time," but when I skipped into the house chanting her words Aunt Elvara slapped my face. Since when was it wrong to sing?

Another place I loved to visit was the grocery store. Its owner was known to be an accomplished thief. A genius. He was so thin that I wondered where he could find the strength to steal as much as a pin. From time to time the police would take him away while his wife shouted, "Don't worry honey, I'll bring you some biscuits." After a brief stay in jail, he would be back again, squatting on his heels in the rear of the store, shooting dice with his friends.

Across the street stood a church. It had once been the home of a friend of my family's, but after the husband had shot his wife to death the Reverend took the house over. On Saturdays the building was used to sell everything from old clothes to baked goods, with the proceeds going to the desperately poor. Some people thought it was scandalous to worship God in the home of a murdered woman, but I liked the new church better than the old one, which had been located in a former grocery store and had a sign above the door saying: "Those who wash their feet before entering are God's children." I detested washing my feet. So I preferred praying in the house of the dead lady. The Reverend was very stern with my friends and me. "If you don't keep still, I'll smack you on the head with my Bible," he'd say, glowering. We would slip down the aisle looking for seats close to where the new converts made their public confessions. The women wore their Sunday dresses and flowered hats.

"Brothers and sisters, we are all God's children! Live and let live. If you give our Lord a nickel, he will give you back five!" the Reverend intoned. Then the collection box was passed. We children never had a cent to offer, but we feared to dip our fingers into the tempting pile of coins since God was watching. Suddenly someone was singing and the crowd hummed along; now feet began to tap and a fat woman in tears was confessing her sins. The singing and stamping of feet grew louder. A man, shouting that he was possessed by the devil, rose to his feet, followed by another and another until the entire congregation was standing, rocking, swaying, eyes closed in ecstasy. A woman fainted and was revived by a friend while the worshippers leaped and twirled, kicking up their feet to drive away the devil, and the Reverend tugged at skirts raised immodestly high. Dizzy with excitement, I felt the call of the Holy Spirit and threw up my legs with the others . . . until the Reverend thundered with God-like wrath: "Everybody out! The service is over. God be with you. . . ."

Margaret: We were very poor. Josephine has mentioned how we were forced to look for food in white men's garbage. Mama was pleased when we brought home a chicken head to put in the soup. It was so cold in winter that our school was forced to close. This delighted Josephine, who was constantly in trouble with the teacher for making faces. "Why is it wrong?" she would ask. "If God gave us faces, he meant us to use them." She was very conscious of her responsibilities as the oldest child and constantly looked for ways to earn money. With the rest of us in tow, she would ring doorbells in the white quarter and offer our services. "Would you like us to shovel your front walk, ma'am? Can we wash your steps? Do you need help waxing your kitchen floor?" Doors were often slammed in her face because of her frail appearance. But when she was told, "You're too little to work, child," she glibly lied: "I know I look young, but I'm really fifteen." When we did get hired we earned from five cents to a quarter, depending on our employer's generosity. Enough to buy an occasional doughnut each. Then we'd set off on a coal hunt. Josephine had organized the neighborhood children into a team. Armed with one of the coal sacks Daddy used to make shoes, we'd head for the railroad yard, where Josephine would jump onto a coal car, agile as a cat. "Be careful. The watchman has a gun!" While one of us stood guard, the rest would gather up the coal Josephine threw us to stuff in our sack. She would still be tossing down chunks when the train began humming and throbbing. "Be careful, Tumpy!" Josephine never jumped until the train was in motion. Our sack was full. Now we would try to sell it.

Josephine: Most of our coal was bought by Mrs. Dullie, a hard-headed woman, half of whose face had somehow been horribly burned. She wore her hair in tiny braids that bristled from her head, in order, I assumed, to lengthen her hair. But in all the time I knew her, her hair never grew an inch. Happy or sad, Mrs. Dullie smiled constantly, flashing the gold teeth that proclaimed her wealth. In spite of her riches, however, she held the neighborhood record for prison terms, having served seven or eight. No one except a policeman with a summons dared to cross her, partly because she was a big, strong woman whose shoes were tipped with intimidating "bulldog" toes and partly because she carried a gun in her pocket. Mrs. Dullie was famous for her home-cooked specialties. No one could match her sandwiches filled with hot, peppered sowbelly and sold with a beer chaser. As her supplier, however, I also knew about the putrid chicken parts she slipped into her pot. After soaking these smelly morsels in salted water laced with bicarbonate of soda to eliminate the odor, she cooked them several hours, then rolled them in dough. Mrs. Dullie's hot pies were big Sunday sellers. . . .

Margaret: In 1918, we left the poorest section of the black quarter for a sturdy cement house with a real cellar. Daddy picked up odd jobs wherever he could and Mama worked in Cousin Josephine's laundry. We children made deliveries for "Aunt Jo" after school in return for the pennies she produced from a pouch beneath her skirts. The rest of the time Tumpy put on shows in our cellar, where she had made a theater like the one at Mrs. Mason's house.

This new theater had an added refinement: candles placed in tin cans to give the effect of footlights. Wearing Grandma's cast-off dresses, Josephine would sweep regally across the stage. "Every show is alike, Tumpy," Richard and I would complain. "We're not coming tonight." Profiting from her age and height, Tumpy would furiously shove us down the cellar steps, snapping, "Get in there and take a seat. If you move, I'll slap your faces." She continued to charge a pin for admission and her friends seemed to like the show, because they kept coming back.

One night the performance ended badly. Tumpy was twirling across the stage when her skirt brushed a candle and her dress caught fire. Screaming with fear, we children rushed upstairs for help. Fortunately a neighbor had the presence of mind to wrap our star in the stage curtain, extinguishing the flames. Grandma's dress was ruined but Tumpy was unharmed. The next day she was out in the street rounding up an audience for the evening show. Dancing was in her blood. "Can't you sit still for a minute?" I'd ask. "This is the best way I know to keep warm," she'd reply.

With fifteen cents of our delivery money we would regularly buy tickets for the Sunday show at the Booker T. Washington Theater, where a vaudeville troupe called the Dixie Steppers performed before a black audience. Every show looked the same to me, but week after week Josephine sat glued to the edge of her seat as chorus girls flashed hints of bare skin, comics made faces and a fat singer in a red wig sang the blues. One day Tumpy announced, "I'm going to talk to the director. Since we're going to have to work someplace, why not in show business? Wouldn't that be fun?" "Not for me," I replied, but Josephine, with an assurance that made me shiver, marched over to the guard at the stage door and announced that she had an appointment to audition. The watchman looked her over from head to toe . . . and let her pass, while I waited trembling outside. A few minutes later, Tumpy was back, beaming and snapping her fingers. "It worked. I'm hired!" I couldn't believe my ears. Just like that? "They were in the middle of a rehearsal," Tumpy explained, "but a nice lady asked what I wanted. 'I'd like to see the director, ma'am,' I replied. She burst out laughing and shouted, 'Bob! You have a caller!'" A very tall, very black man with white hair and a kind face had asked, "What do you want, child?" "Please, mister, could you give me a job?" "But you're much too young." "I may look small, but I'm really fifteen." So Tumpy had pulled her usual trick! Maybe it worked for shoveling snow, but in the theater? . . . "He asked if I knew how to dance." "For once you could tell the truth." "No, I lied to him. I said I couldn't dance a step but I hoped he would teach me." "But you *can* dance, Tumpy!" "Not as well as the chorus line. Anyway, this way he'll have a surprise. I start rehearsing tomorrow."

The next day I followed Tumpy through the stage door, as cool as a nine-year-old could be. Tumpy showed me around as if she had lived backstage for years, pointing out the strips of painted canvas rolled out on the floor and the instruments piled into corners. "Do they know you can play the trombone, Tumpy?" "No, but they hired me anyway."

Tumpy's experience with the trombone had been short-lived. A musician couple, the Joneses, used to perform in our neighborhood restaurants as the Jones Family Band. There were actually three of them: Mr. Jones, who was very small and ugly, his tall, pretty wife and their daughter, Doll, who luckily took after her mother. The Joneses asked Mama if Tumpy could join their act. Her pay would be the free meals the band received from the restaurants in which they performed. My sister was very excited at the idea of learning to play a real instrument, but in spite of the fact that Mr. Jones taught her to play the trombone, she soon was home again, worn out and thinner than ever. The Joneses walked miles a day from job to job and Mr. Jones had made Tumpy carry the property trunk.

We stood in the wings watching the chorus line rehearse. I knew how high Tumpy could kick, but these dancers moved in such perfect lines! "Look at their faces," Tumpy said with a sniff. "Not a single smile. Wait until I get my turn." But it wasn't to be that day. "Come back tomorrow," said Mr. Bob Russell. Was he trying to discourage her? If so, he didn't know my sister. The next day we were there in the wings again. "All right, child, get out there with the others," Mr. Russell ordered. The piano player struck a few notes and Tumpy began to dance, but not at all like the rest. Her body moved as though it were on fire. Mr. Russell clapped his hands to stop the music and I thought that Tumpy was finished for good. Some of the chorus girls were sneering and laughing and pointing at Josephine. But Mr. Russell put a quick stop to that. "I have just the part for you," he said. "You'll be our Cupid. Report for rehearsal tomorrow."

We decided not to breathe a word to our parents. If Mama found out that Tumpy was appearing on the stage with half-naked chorus girls, my sister would get a good whipping. Instead we said we were playing in a friend's basement since the fire had scared us away from our own. Our parents were used to our roaming the neighborhood.

On Josephine's opening night, I sat in the audience, heart in mouth. The curtain rose to reveal two lovers standing on a little balcony. Suddenly Tumpy flitted across the stage, a smiling angel in baggy pink tights, complete with two little wings, a quiver and arrows. I thought she looked beautiful and admired the courage with which she hung suspended from the ceiling, the symbol of romantic love. The audience gasped with delight, but their pleasure quickly changed to concern. Just as the piano player burst into a series of tremolos, one of Cupid's wings hooked onto the backdrop, leaving Tumpy wriggling in space. A stagehand, hoping to help, tried to adjust the scenery but only succeeded in getting Cupid stuck for good. "Raise the backdrop," the director shouted, but to no avail. Love's Messenger continued to wave her legs in the air while the couple on the balcony proclaimed everlasting love.

To my surprise, the audience roared with laughter, slapping their thighs and flashing their teeth, while the wronged husband, right on cue, rushed onto the stage to separate his wife from her lover. . . . It seemed like hours before the curtain finally descended.

I huddled in my seat, mortified. Mr. Russell stood glaring in the wings, Tumpy told me later, but his expression quickly changed when someone rushed backstage to announce that the scene had been a triumph. The audience had never laughed so hard and many of the spectators wanted seats for the next performance. Tumpy, her eyes filled with tears, didn't dare face Mr. Russell. "Don't worry, child," he said gently. "There's another show tomorrow and from now on you'll get stuck *on purpose.*" The theater was full for days.

Josephine was delighted with her success, but as time went on her mood changed. The show would soon be leaving town. One Saturday we set off as usual to buy the family's Sunday fish. I could tell there was something wrong. Finally Tumpy blurted out, "Margaret, before I say another word I want you to cross your heart. Good. Now swear that you won't tell Mama—I'm leaving town tomorrow with the show." "No, Tumpy. You can't." Wrapping her arms around me, Josephine tried to explain. She could never become a famous star if she stayed in St. Louis. And being famous meant earning lots of money, never being poor again, helping the family. It also meant showing whites what blacks could do and proving that we're all God's children. Wasn't that true? Surely I understood. I had to agree, but the thought of Tumpy's absence was hard to bear. . . . Nevertheless, I had crossed my heart. My sister hugged me until I was breathless. When had she become so strong? Then she disappeared into the dusk.

I returned home alone, clutching the fish. Nobody noticed Josephine's absence at first, but when night came, Mama asked, "Where's Tumpy?" "She stopped by Mrs. Dayan's house," I replied. Mrs. Dayan was a family friend who lived some distance away. "Since it's so late, she'll probably stay the night," Grandma said. The next day, however, when Tumpy had still not returned, there was talk of calling the police. From the way I hung my head, Mama knew I was hiding something. I finally burst into tears and confessed. To my surprise, Mama calmed Grandma and quietly said, "She has chosen her path. Let her be." "Perhaps it's God's will," Grandma added.

I thought often of my sister, with a mixture of pain and envy. It was true. She had made her choice: chosen to turn her back on Tumpy and all the rest of her childhood to become Josephine. With nothing for baggage but the dress on her back and one pair of shoes, she had set out to conquer the world. She was thirteen years old.

30

LANGSTON HUGHES

The Big Sea: An Autobiography
1940

The childhood of Langston Hughes (1902–1967), who would later become one of the best-known poets of the Harlem Renaissance, was somewhat more comfortable than Josephine Baker's, but it was similarly limited by the color of his skin. Hughes was born in Joplin, Missouri, raised in Lawrence, Kansas, and attended high school in Cleveland. The excerpts from his autobiography describe his years at Central High School in Cleveland, which he attended in the 1910s, during the time of the Great Migration of African Americans from the South to northern cities.

I had no sooner graduated from grammar school in Lincoln than we moved from Illinois to Cleveland. My step-father sent for us. He was

Langston Hughes, *The Big Sea: An Autobiography* (New York: Hill and Wang, 1940), 26–30, 32–33, 52–53.

working in a steel mill during the war, and making lots of money. But it was hard work, and he never looked the same afterwards. Every day he worked several hours overtime, because they paid well for overtime. But after a while, he couldn't stand the heat of the furnaces, so he got a job as caretaker of a theater building, and after that as janitor of an apartment house.

Rents were very high for colored people in Cleveland, and the Negro district was extremely crowded, because of the great migration. It was difficult to find a place to live. We always lived, during my high school years, either in an attic or a basement, and paid quite a lot for such inconvenient quarters. White people on the east side of the city were moving out of their frame houses and renting them to Negroes at double and triple the rents they could receive from others. An eight-room house with one bath would be cut up into apartments and five or six families crowded into it, each two-room kitchenette apartment renting for what the whole house had rented for before.

But Negroes were coming in in a great dark tide from the South, and they had to have some place to live. Sheds and garages and store fronts were turned into living quarters. As always, the white neighborhoods resented Negroes moving closer and closer—but when the whites did give way, they gave way at very profitable rentals. So most of the colored people's wages went for rent. The landlords and the banks made it difficult for them to buy houses, so they had to pay the exorbitant rents required. When my step-father quit the steel mill job, my mother went out to work in service to help him meet expenses. She paid a woman four dollars a week to take care of my little brother while she worked as a maid.

I went to Central High School in Cleveland. We had a magazine called the *Belfry Owl*. I wrote poems for the *Belfry Owl*. We had some wise and very good teachers, Miss Roberts and Miss Weimer in English, Miss Chesnutt, who was the daughter of the famous colored writer, Charles W. Chesnutt, and Mr. Hitchcock, who taught geometry with humor, and Mr. Ozanne, who spread the whole world before us in his history classes. Also Clara Dieke, who painted beautiful pictures and who taught us a great deal about many things that are useful to know—about law and order in art and life, and about sticking to a thing until it is done. . . .

Central was the high school of students of foreign-born parents—until the Negroes came. It is an old high school with many famous graduates. It used to be long ago the high school of the aristocrats, until the aristocrats moved farther out. Then poor whites and foreign-born took over the district. Then during the war, the Negroes came.

Now Central is almost entirely a Negro school in the heart of Cleveland's vast Negro quarter.

When I was there, it was very nearly entirely a foreign-born school, with a few native white and colored American students mixed in. By foreign, I mean children of foreign-born parents. Although some of the students themselves had been born in Poland or Russia, Hungary or Italy. And most were Catholic or Jewish.

Although we got on very well, whenever class elections would come up, there was a distinct Jewish-Gentile division among my classmates. That was perhaps why I held many class and club offices in high school, because often when there was a religious deadlock, a Negro student would win the election. They would compromise on a Negro, feeling, I suppose, that a Negro was neither Jew nor Gentile!

I wore a sweater covered with club pins most of the time. I was on the track team, and for two seasons, my relay team won the city-wide championships. I was a lieutenant in the military training corps. Once or twice I was on the monthly honor roll for scholarship. And when we were graduated, Class of '20, I edited the Year Book. . . .

The second summer vacation [from high school] I went to join my mother in Chicago. Dad and my mother were separated again, and she was working as cook for a lady who owned a millinery shop in the Loop, a very fashionable shop where society leaders came by appointment and hats were designed to order. I became a delivery boy for that shop. It was a terrifically hot summer, and we lived on the crowded Chicago South Side in a house next to the elevated. The thunder of the trains kept us awake at night. We could afford only one small room for my mother, my little brother, and me.

South State Street was in its glory then, a teeming Negro street with crowded theaters, restaurants, and cabarets. And excitement from noon to noon. Midnight was like day. The street was full of workers and gamblers, prostitutes and pimps, church folks and sinners. The tenements on either side was very congested. For neither love nor money could you find a decent place to live. Profiteers, thugs, and gangsters were coming into their own. The first Sunday I was in town, I went out walking alone to see what the city looked like. I wandered too far outside the Negro district, over beyond Wentworth, and was set upon and beaten by a group of white boys, who said they didn't allow niggers in that neighborhood. I came home with both eyes blacked and a swollen jaw. That was the summer before the Chicago riots.

I managed to save a little money, so I went back to high school in Cleveland, leaving my mother in Chicago. I couldn't afford to eat in a restaurant, and the only thing I knew how to cook myself in the kitchen of the house where I roomed was rice, which I boiled to a paste. Rice and hot dogs, rice and hot dogs, every night for dinner. Then I read myself to sleep. . . .

My father raised my allowance that year, so I was able to help my mother with the expenses of our household. It was a pleasant year for me, for I was a senior. I was elected Class Poet and Editor of our Year Book. As an officer in the drill corps, I wore a khaki uniform and leather puttees, and gave orders. I went calling on a little brownskin girl, who was as old as I was—seventeen—but only in junior high school, because she had just come up from the poor schools of the South. I met her at a dance at the Longwood Gym. She had big eyes and skin like rich chocolate. Sometimes she wore a red dress that was very becoming to her, so I wrote a poem about her that declared:

> When Susanna Jones wears red
> Her face is like an ancient cameo
> Turned brown by the ages.
>
> Come with a blast of trumpets,
> Jesus!
>
> When Susanna Jones wears red
> A queen from some time-dead Egyptian night
> Walks once again.
>
> Blow trumpets, Jesus!
> And the beauty of Susanna Jones in red
> Burns in my heart a love-fire sharp like pain.
>
> Sweet silver trumpets,
> Jesus!

I had a whole notebook full of poems by now, and another one full of verses and jingles. I always tried to keep verses and poems apart, although I saw no harm in writing verses if you felt like it, and poetry if you could.

June came. And graduation. Like most graduations, it made you feel both sorry and glad: sorry to be leaving and glad to be going.

A Chronology of Child Welfare Reforms in the Progressive Era (1853–1938)

1853 Charles Loring Brace founds the Children's Aid Society in New York City.

1860 Reformers in Hartford, Connecticut, establish the first Boys Club.

1867 The first installment of Horatio Alger's first rags-to-riches story begins running in *The Student and Schoolmate*. It was later published as *Ragged Dick, or, Street Life in New York*.

1870 U.S. Census first records child labor.

1872 Charles Loring Brace publishes *The Dangerous Classes of New York, and Twenty Years' Work among Them,* a memoir of his work in New York's slums.

1874 New York Society for the Prevention of Cruelty to Children established.

New York City Department of Health distributes infant care and diphtheria leaflets.

1878 First free kindergarten in the East founded in New York City.

1888 American Pediatric Association founded.

1889 Jane Addams and Ellen Gates Starr found Hull House, the famous social settlement on the West Side of Chicago.

1892 Jacob Riis, the photographer and social reformer, publishes *The Children of the Poor,* an exposé of the harsh living conditions of children in the ghettos of New York City.

John Gunckel establishes the Toledo Newsboys' Association, one of the most successful organizations of its type in the country.

1893 Lillian Wald establishes the Henry Street Settlement in Lower Manhattan.

1894   The Child Study Association begins applying social scientific research methods to the study of child development.

Boston begins requiring medical inspections of school children.

Luther Emmett Holt publishes *The Care and Feeding of Children,* one of the most popular "modern" child-rearing guides.

1895   William George establishes the first junior republic, a self-governing camp for city youth, at Freeville, near Ithaca, New York.

1899   The first juvenile court in the United States is established in Chicago.

Connecticut is the first state to require medical inspections and eye tests of children.

1900   About 8 percent of all children in the United States between the ages of fourteen and seventeen attend high school.

The Swedish author and educator Ellen Key publishes *The Century of the Child.*

1902   New York City begins the first school nursing program.

1904   The National Child Labor Committee, the first effective lobbying group for reforming child labor conditions, is established.

G. Stanley Hall publishes the influential *Adolescence: Its Psychology and Its Relations to Physiology, Anthropology, Sociology, Sex, Crime, Religion, and Education.*

1905   Florence Kelley publishes *Some Ethical Gains through Legislation,* in which she declares that all children should have "a right to childhood."

The first theater devoted solely to presenting moving pictures opens in Pittsburgh. Its first feature is *The Great Train Robbery.*

1906   The Federated Boys Clubs (later Boys Clubs of America and, later, the Boys and Girls Clubs of America) is formed.

The Massachusetts legislature passes the nation's first school health law.

Jacob Riis, Jane Addams, Lillian Wald, and others form the Playground Association of America.

1908   The Juvenile Protective Association is formed to promote juvenile courts, junior republics, and other child welfare activities.

New York City establishes a child hygiene division in its city health department, the first in the United States.

Boston establishes the first "fresh air" school for children suffering from tuberculosis and other respiratory problems.

1909   More than two hundred reformers attend a White House conference to discuss the care and management of the 150,000 orphaned and institutionalized children in the United States.

1910   New York City begins serving school lunches.

The Boy Scouts of America is established.

The Mann Act outlaws interstate transportation of girls and women for immoral purposes.

1911   The Camp Fire Girls is established.

Illinois becomes first state to create pensions for widows with dependent children.

The Safety Institute of America is founded. It publishes safety guides for adults and children, and lobbies for playgrounds and other recreational opportunities for children.

Child welfare exhibits are held in New York and Chicago.

1912   The U.S. Children's Bureau, the first federal agency devoted expressly to the welfare of children, is founded with Julia Lathrop as director.

The Girl Scouts of America is established.

1916   The U.S. Congress passes and President Woodrow Wilson signs the Keating-Owens Act, the first federal legislation regulating child labor.

Lewis Terman, a psychologist at Stanford, develops the intelligence quotient, a measurement of IQ that will be used to test children for decades.

1917   In *Hammer v. Dagenhart,* the U.S. Supreme Court declares the Keating-Owens Act unconstitutional.

1919   The White House Conference on Child Welfare Standards establishes standards for child employment, children's health and welfare, and medical care for infants and mothers.

1920   About 32 percent of all children between the ages of fourteen and seventeen attend high school.

1921   Congress passes the Sheppard-Towner Act, which provides for the gathering of statistics on prenatal care and infant mortality.

1922   The International Council of Women issues its Children's Charter, which proposes the development of a set of minimum rights for children throughout the world.

1926   On May 1, "No Accident Day" is held in New York City, honoring the memory of the 7,000 boys and girls killed nationwide in traffic accidents in 1925.

1930   Delegates to a White House conference issue the Children's Charter, a set of nineteen principles on health, education, child labor, recreation, and the family.

1938   President Franklin Roosevelt signs the Fair Labor Standards Act into law. It prohibits the employment of children under the age of sixteen.

Questions for Consideration

1. How did children's perceptions of the city differ from adults' perceptions of the city?

2. How did reformers' attitudes about immigrants and about the poor change between the 1880s and the 1920s? How did they remain the same?

3. What motivated reformers to try to improve the lives of city children?

4. In what ways did religion affect the lives of urban children and the programs designed by child welfare reformers?

5. What were the greatest dangers facing urban children? What opportunities did cities provide for them?

6. How did society view the sexuality of urban youth? How did adults' concern about the "boy problem" differ from their concern about the "girl problem"? How were the solutions they proposed for these problems different?

7. How were the experiences and attitudes of African American and immigrant children different from those of white, "native-born" children? How were they the same? What can you determine about the state of race relations in the United States based on the reports and activities of child welfare reformers?

8. What roles did new technologies—the automobile and movies, to name just two examples—play in the lives of urban children?

9. What kinds of paid labor did children and teenagers perform early in the twentieth century? How were child labor laws supposed to improve the lives of working children?

10. Why did "child savers" create separate legal systems for juveniles who broke the law? Did juvenile courts accomplish what their creators hoped they would?

11. Improving health care was one of the chief priorities for child welfare reformers. What practices and institutions did reformers advocate to extend and improve the lives of children?

12. How was education used to improve the lives of city children? What new methods of teaching and learning were introduced during the Progressive Era?

13. How did child-rearing practices vary according to class and ethnicity?

14. How did society's expectations for children and youth differ during this period from the expectations contemporary society has for youth today?

15. Which of the problems facing urban children in the early twentieth century still exist in the early twenty-first century? How are modern child welfare institutions and organizations different or similar to the institutions and organizations of the Progressive Era?

Selected Bibliography

Alexander, Ruth M. *The Girl Problem: Female Sexual Delinquency in New York, 1900–1930.* Ithaca, N.Y.: Cornell University Press, 1995.

Ashby, LeRoy. *Endangered Children: Dependency, Neglect, and Abuse in American History.* New York: Twayne Publishers, 1997.

Berrol, Selma Cantor. *Growing Up American: Immigrant Children in America, Then and Now.* New York: Twayne Publishers, 1995.

Brumberg, Stephan. *Going to America, Going to School: The Jewish Immigrant Public School Encounter in Turn-of-the-Century New York City.* New York: Praeger, 1986.

Bullough, William. *Cities and Schools in the Gilded Age: The Evolution of an Urban Institution.* Port Washington, N.Y.: Kennikat Press, 1974.

Cavallo, Dominick. *Muscles and Morals: Organized Playgrounds and Urban Reform, 1880–1920.* Philadelphia: University of Pennsylvania Press, 1981.

Clapp, Elizabeth J. *Mothers of All Children: Women Reformers and the Rise of Juvenile Courts in Progressive Era America.* University Park: Pennsylvania State University Press, 1998.

Clement, Priscilla Ferguson. *Growing Pains: Children of the Industrial Age, 1850–1890.* New York: Twayne Publishers, 1997.

Cmiel, Kenneth. *A Home of Another Kind: One Chicago Orphanage and the Tangle of Child Welfare.* Chicago: University of Chicago Press, 1995.

Cohen, Ronald D. *Children of the Mill: Schooling and Society in Gary, Indiana, 1906–1960.* Bloomington: Indiana University Press, 1990.

Crenson, Matthew A. *Building the Invisible Orphanage: A Prehistory of the American Welfare System.* Cambridge: Harvard University Press, 1998.

Cross, Gary. *Kids' Stuff: Toys and the Changing World of American Childhood.* Cambridge: Harvard University Press, 1997.

Davis, Allen F. *Spearheads for Reform: The Social Settlements and the Progressive Movement, 1890–1914.* New York: Oxford University Press, 1967.

Denning, Michael. *Mechanic Accents: Dime Novels and Working-Class Culture in America.* New York: Verso, 1987.

Fass, Paula. *The Damned and the Beautiful: American Youth in the 1920s.* New York: Oxford University Press, 1977.

———. *Kidnapped: Child Abduction in America*. Cambridge: Harvard University Press, 1997.

Flanagan, Maureen A. *Seeing with Their Hearts: Chicago Women and the Vision of the Good City, 1871–1933*. Princeton, N.J.: Princeton University Press, 2002.

Formanek-Brunell, Miriam. *Made to Play House: Dolls and the Commercialization of American Girlhood, 1830–1930*. New Haven, Conn.: Yale University Press, 1993.

Gould, Lewis L. *America in the Progressive Era, 1890–1914*. London: Pearson Education, 2001.

Graff, Harvey J. *Conflicting Paths: Growing Up in America*. Cambridge: Harvard University Press, 1995.

Hawes, Joseph. *Children in Urban Society: Juvenile Delinquency in Nineteenth-Century America*. New York: Oxford University Press, 1971.

Hindman, Hugh D. *Child Labor: An American History*. Armonk, N.Y.: M. E. Sharpe, 2002.

Holl, Jack M. *Juvenile Reform in the Progressive Era: William R. George and the Junior Republic Movement*. Ithaca, N.Y.: Cornell University Press, 1971.

Holoran, Peter C. *Boston's Wayward Children: Social Services for Homeless Children, 1830–1930*. Rutherford, N.J.: Fairleigh Dickinson University Press, 1989.

Holt, Marilyn Irvin. *The Orphan Trains: Placing Out in America*. Lincoln: University of Nebraska Press, 1992.

Illick, Joseph E. *American Childhoods*. Philadelphia: University of Pennsylvania Press, 2002.

Kasson, John F. *Amusing the Millions: Coney Island at the Turn of the Century*. New York: Hill & Wang, 1978.

Kunzel, Regina G. *Fallen Women, Problem Girls: Unmarried Mothers and the Professionalization of Social Work, 1890–1940*. New Haven, Conn.: Yale University Press, 1993.

Labaree, David F. *The Making of an American High School: The Credentials Market and the Central High School of Philadelphia*. New Haven, Conn.: Yale University Press, 1988.

Lindenmeyer, Kriste. *A Right to Childhood: The U.S. Children's Bureau and Child Welfare, 1912–1946*. Urbana: University of Illinois Press, 1997.

Macleod, David I. *Building Character in the American Boy: The Boy Scouts, YMCA, and Their Forerunners, 1870–1920*. Madison: University of Wisconsin Press, 1983.

———. *The Age of the Child: Children in America, 1890–1920*. New York: Twayne Publishers, 1998.

McGerr, Michael. *A Fierce Discontent: The Rise and Fall of the Progressive Movement in America, 1870–1920*. New York: Free Press, 2003.

Meckel, Richard A. *Save the Babies: American Public Health Reform and the Prevention of Infant Mortality, 1850–1929.* Baltimore: Johns Hopkins University Press, 1990.

Mennel, Robert. *Thorns and Thistles: Juvenile Delinquents in the United States.* Hanover, N.H.: University Press of New England, 1973.

Nasaw, David. *Schooled to Order: A Social History of Public Schooling in the United States.* New York: Oxford University Press, 1979.

———. *Children of the City: At Work and at Play.* New York: Oxford University Press, 1985.

Perlman, Joel. *Ethnic Differences: Schooling and Social Structure among the Irish, Italians, Jews, and Blacks in an American City, 1880–1935.* Cambridge, England: Cambridge University Press, 1988.

Reese, William J. *The Origins of the American High School.* New Haven, Conn.: Yale University Press, 1995.

Sanders, James W. *The Education of an Urban Minority: Catholics in Chicago, 1833–1965.* New York: Oxford University Press, 1977.

Sealander, Judith. *The Failed Century of the Child: Governing America's Young in the Twentieth Century.* New York: Cambridge University Press, 2003.

Skocpol, Theda. *Protecting Soldiers and Mothers: The Political Origins of Social Policy in the United States.* Cambridge: Harvard University Press, 1992.

Tiffin, Susan. *In Whose Best Interest? Child Welfare Reform in the Progressive Era.* Westport, Conn.: Greenwood Press, 1982.

Trattner, Walter. *Crusade for the Children: A History of the National Child Labor Committee and Child Labor Reform in America.* Chicago: Quadrangle Books, 1970.

Ueda, Reed. *Avenues to Adulthood: The Origins of the High School and Social Mobility in an American Suburb.* New York: Cambridge University Press, 1987.

West, Elliott. *Growing Up in Twentieth-Century America: A History and Reference Guide.* Westport, Conn.: Greenwood Press, 1996.

Willrich, Michael. *City of Courts: Socializing Justice in Progressive Era Chicago.* New York: Cambridge University Press, 2003.

Zelizer, Viviana A. *Pricing the Priceless Child: The Changing Social Value of Children.* New York: Basic Books, 1985.

Acknowledgments

Golda Meir, from *My Life* by Golda Meir, copyright © 1975 by Golda Meir. Used by permission of G. P. Putnam's Sons, a division of Penguin Group (USA) Inc.

Josephine Baker, "Josephine." English translation copyright © 1977 by Harper & Row, Publishers, Inc. Reprinted by permission of HarperCollins Publishers Inc.

Langston Hughes, from *The Big Sea, An Autobiography.* Copyright © by Langston Hughes. Copyright renewed 1968 by Anna Bontemps and George Houston Bass. Reprinted by permission of Hill and Wang, a division of Farrar, Straus and Giroux, LLC.

Index

abortion, 90
accidental deaths, 8, 174
Addams, Jane, 1, 4, 14, 23, 91, 172, 173
"Spirit of Youth and the City Streets,
The," 39–43
*Adolescence: Its Psychology and Its Relations
to Physiology, Anthropology, Sociology,
Sex, Crime, Religion, and Education*
(Hall), 173
affluent children, 92–93
African Americans
Baker, Josephine, memoir, 161–68
civil rights of, 93
community schools, 107–14
discrimination against, 169
Hughes, Langston, memoir, 168–71
Little Mothers, 103
Progressive reforms and, viii
prostitution and, 46–47
school athletics, 56–57
school attendance, 169–70
school discipline of, 51–52
school race relations, 49–59
teachers, attitudes toward, 52–53
terminology, viii
voluntary grouping of, 54, 56
alcohol problems, 34–35, 37, 41
Alcott, Bronson, 91
Alcott, Louisa May, 91*n*
American Pediatric Association, 172
American Young Sisters Society, 160
amusement parks, 7
Astyanax, 92
athletics, race and, 56–57
automobiles
boys' problems and, 59–60
traffic accidents, 8, 174

babies. *See* infant care
baby contests, 16
"baby tents," 15, 131–35
baby week campaigns, 16
Baker, Josephine
"Josephine," 161–68

Baker, Margaret, 162–68
basket sellers, 69
bathing infants, 105–6, 134
beads, linking and wiring, 72
beer, fed to babies, 10
Belfry Owl, 169
Berger, Victor, 159
"better mothers" contests, 16
Big Brothers, 19
"Big Sea, The: An Autobiography"
(Hughes), 168–71
Big Sisters, 19
blindness prevention, 130–31
bluestocking, 158
Bogardus, Emory S.
"City Boy and His Problems, The: A Survey of Life in Los Angeles," 59–63
Boston Association for the Relief and Control of Tuberculosis, 99–102
Boston English high school, 22
Boston School Board, 99–102
bottle feeding, 133–34
Bowers, Claude G., 23, 25
"boy problem." *See* juvenile delinquency
boys. *See also* juvenile delinquency
"animal spirits of," 126
automobile and, 59–60
"boy problem," 17–21
character building, 128, 141
clubs and organizations for, 18, 112–13,
127–28
cotton industry, 80, 84*f*
focus on, viii
gangs, 126, 127
juvenile delinquency and, 16–21
living conditions of, 32
paths to juvenile delinquency, 149–55
reforms for, 127–28
street work, 32
trade schools for, 35
vocational education for, 110
Boys and Girls Clubs of America, 173
Boys' Brotherhood Republic, 18
Boys Clubs of America, 18, 172, 173

183

Boy Scouts of America, 19, 127–28, 174
Brace, Charles Loring, 14, 172
    "Dangerous Classes of New York, and
        Twenty Years' Work among Them,"
        30–33
Buffalo Bill's "Wild West Show," 13
bullies, newsboys and, 65–66
burglary, by children/youth, 115–16, 153,
    155. *See also* juvenile delinquency

cabarets, 60
"Caddy Camp," 19
calomel, 118
Camp Fire Girls, 19, 113, 174
Captains Courageous (Kipling), 92
carding jewelry, 72
carding shoe buttons, 72, 74
carding snaps, 71–72, 74
Care and Feeding of Children, The (Holt),
    173
carpenter shops, school, 109
case studies, 93–106
Century of the Child, The (Key), 173
chain fastener assembly, 72, 75
chaperonage, 42
character
    building in boys, 128, 141
    of newsboys, 141–45
Charities and the Commons, 12, 89, 93,
    100
Chesnutt, Charles W., 169
Chicago
    child welfare efforts in, 14–15
    Health Department, 1
    juvenile justice system, 114, 117–22
    tenements, 170
    Vice Commission, 43–44, 146
Chicago Child Welfare Exhibit, 1–2,
    123–39, 174
    displays, 123–24, 136
    "Child Health and Welfare," 129–36
    "Images from the Chicago Child Welfare
        Exhibit," 136–39
    interest in, 124
    "Introductory Remarks" (McCormick),
        124–26
    posters, 136–39
    "Team Work for City Boys," 126–28
Chicago Commission on Race Relations
    "Negro in Chicago, The: A Study of
        Race Relations and a Race Riot,"
        49–59
"Chicago Juvenile Court, The" (Jeter),
    117–22
Chicago School of Civics and Philanthropy,
    Social Investigation Dept., 48
Chicago *Tribune,* 10
child care. *See also* infant care
    education of Little Mothers on, 104–6
    poverty and, 16
    traditional, 39–40

"Child Health and Welfare" (Chicago Child
    Welfare Exhibit), 129–36
childhood illness. *See also* health
    Child Welfare Exhibit on, 1–2
    in detention homes, 118–19
    epidemics, 9–10
    health care and, 97–98
    preventable, 1–2, 129, 130
child labor. *See also* employment; street
        trades
    campaign against, 21–22
    children's rights and, 91–92
    earnings, 9, 65, 68, 69, 70, 71, 72, 74–76,
        112
    eyesight and, 131
    girls, 32, 40, 43–49, 65, 71, 78–81, 82–83*f*
    "home workers," 8, 9, 71–76, 87*f*
    machine work, 76–78
    newspaper sales, 8
    photographic documentation of, 81–87
    poster, 138*f*
    research on, 11
    "street trades," 8–9, 64–70
    studies, 63–87
    in working-class families, 8–9
    working conditions, 8, 64–78
Child Labor Bulletin
    "Story of My Cotton Dress, The," 79–81
child labor laws, 173
    Keating-Owen Act, 22, 174
    Progressive interest in, 3
    rationale for, 70, 91–92
    studies supporting, 63
    working conditions and, 8
child mortality, 2, 8, 129. *See also* health
    infant mortality, 9–10, 132, 174
    rates in urban areas, 9–10, 34
    rights of children and, 91
"child-nurture" philosophy, 6
children. *See also* immigrant children;
        urban children/youth
    of affluent Americans, 92–93
    attitudes toward, 5–6
    development of, 104–6, 173
    economic value of, 8, 89
    education of, 22–24
    family size, 6–8
    importance of, 124–26
    Progressive reforms and, vii–viii
    spirit of, 39–43
    youth culture, 22–25
Children of the Poor (Riis), 172
"Children on the Streets of Cincinnati"
        (Clopper), 64–70
Children's Aid Society, 14, 32–33, 172
Children's Charter
    International Council of Women, 174
    White House conference, 175
children's rights
    importance of children, 124–26
    infant welfare, 132

League of Nations, Declaration of the Rights of the Child, 88
  Progressive views on, 88, 89–93
  right to be born, 90
  right to be happy, 91–92
  right to childhood, 88
  right to grow up, 90–91
  right to rise above parents' level, 92
  right to vocational education, 92
Child-Rescue Campaign, 13
Child Study Association, 173
child welfare
  chronology, 172–75
  conferences, 12–13
  goals of, 124–26
  "heartbreaking conditions," 1–2
  journals, 12
  philanthropy, 123, 124
  poverty and, 10–13
  Progressive interest in, 3
  research on, 11–13
  as a "women's issue," 15
Child Welfare Exhibits, 1–2, 12
  Chicago, 1–2, 123–39, 174
  New York, 174
Child Welfare magazine, 12
child welfare reform
  case studies of, 93–106
  children's rights, 88, 89–93
  middle-class attitudes and, 6–10
  moral indignation and, 4–5
  objectives of, 2
  origins of, vii
  proposed by Children's Aid Society, 32–33
  "right to childhood" and, 88
  small-town nostalgia and, 4
  Social Gospel movement and, 4
child welfare studies, 43–63. *See also* research
  African Americans, 46–47
  boys' problems, 59–63
  juvenile court records analysis, 48–49
  living conditions, 43–49
  race relations, 49–59
  sexual abuse, 48–49
  sexual behavior, 45–46, 47
Cincinnati, Ohio
  child labor conditions, 64–70
  Health Department, 103
  Little Mothers' Movement, 102–6
"City Boy and His Problems: A Survey of Life in Los Angeles, The" (Bogardus), 59–63
"City of Hawthorne, The" (Robinson), 93–98
City Park Association, Philadelphia, 17
Civic Club, Philadelphia, 17
civil rights, 93
Civil War orphans, 14
Cleveland, Ohio
  African American childhood in, 168–71

Cleveland Park Camp Fire, Washington, D.C., 19
Clopper, E. N.
  "Children on the Streets of Cincinnati," 64–70
clothing
  girls' styles, 41
  for infants, 134
coal, children's sale of, 164
cobbling instruction, in school, 110
Colorado "school law," 114
"Commonwealth of Ford," 18
community centers, schools as, 113
conferences, child welfare, 12–13
Cook County (Chicago), Illinois juvenile justice system, 114
cooking classes, in school, 110
cotton industry
  cotton mills, 79, 84*f*
  cutting and sewing dresses, 80–81
  economic value of children in, 89
  picking cotton, 79
  spinning thread, 79–80
  weaving cloth, 80
courtship, 42
crime. *See also* juvenile delinquency
  causes of, 31
  "dangerous classes" and, 30–33
crocheting instruction, in school, 109–10
Cromwell, Oliver, 41
Crosby, Ernest H.
  "Machines, The," 76–78
"Crystallizing Theories into Simple Facts at the Welfare Exhibit, That the First Half May Know How the Other Half Lives," 10
Culture Extension League, Philadelphia, 17

dance halls, 41, 42, 60–61
"dangerous classes," 30–33
"Dangerous Classes of New York, and Twenty Years' Work among Them" (Brace), 30–33
Dangerous Classes of New York, and Twenty Years' Work among Them (Brace), 30, 172
"Dangerous Life, The" (Lindsey), 114–17
Davis, Philip, 4
death
  causes of, 9–10
  child mortality, 2, 8, 9–10, 34, 91, 129
  from preventable diseases, 1–2, 129
  from traffic accidents, 8, 174
Declaration of the Rights of the Child, League of Nations, 88
Delineator, The, 13
dental care, 118–19, 135–36
dependent children, institutions for, 13–14
detention homes, 117–22, 154, 155
  daily routine in, 119–22
  dental care in, 118–19

detention homes (*cont.*)
  health care in, 118–19
  reception of children into, 117–19
  typical cases, 120–22
Devine, Edward T.
  "Right View of the Child, The," 89–93
Dewey, Evelyn, 107
  with Dewey, John, "Schools of Tomor-
    row," 107–14
Dewey, John, 107
  with Dewey, Evelyn, "Schools of Tomor-
    row," 107–14
Dieke, Clara, 169
discipline
  in detention homes, 119–20
  in elementary schools, 51–52
  self-government and, 95–96
doffer boys, 80
domestic science classes, 110–11
Du Bois, W. E. B., 93

earnings
  of basket sellers, 69
  contributed toward family income, 68, 71,
    75–76, 112, 163–64
  of errand boys and girls, 70
  of "home workers," 72, 74–76
  of newsboys, 65
East Side tenements, 7, 34
East St. Louis race riots, 162
education. *See also* health education; voca-
    tional education
  on child care, for Little Mothers, 104–6
  elementary schools, 49–55
  health and hygiene, 15–16, 96–98
  high schools, 22–24, 55–59, 173, 174
  importance of, 161
  lack of, crime and, 31
  Progressive policies, 107–14
  race relations in elementary schools,
    49–55
  race relations in high schools, 55–59
  schools, 106–14
  sex education, 45–46
  trade schools, 35
  vocational, 92
  youth culture, 22–24
elementary schools
  African American teachers in, 52–53
  discipline in, 51–52
  playground race relations, 53
  race relations in, 49–55
employment. *See also* child labor
  odd jobs, 163–64
  summer jobs, 160–61
enfants perdus (lost children), 31
English language learning, 158
entertainment. *See also* recreation
  for children, 7
  in detention homes, 119

moving pictures, 173
show business, 164–68
epidemics, 9–10
epsom salt, 118
errand boys and girls
  earnings, 70
  nationalities of, 69–70
  school attendance by, 70
  working conditions, 69–70
  working hours, 70
eyesight
  of babies, 105
  blindness prevention, 130–31
  child labor and, 131
  eyestrain, from "home work," 72, 73

Fair Labor Standards Act of 1938, 22, 175
families
  contribution of child's income to, 68, 71,
    75–76, 112, 163–64
  "home work" involvement by, 71, 72
  juvenile delinquency and, 149–55
  sexual abuse in, 48–49
  size of, 6–8
fatigue
  in children in cotton industry, 81
  in "home workers," 73–74
Feder, Sarah, 158
federal government, vii, 12–13
Federated Boys' Clubs, 12, 18, 173
Ford Republic, 18
"fresh air" schools, 173
Froebel, Friedrich, 91
fruit venders, 68–69
fundraising, for school textbooks, 159–60

gangs, 126, 127, 151–52
gardening, by children, 101, 112
General Federation of Women's Clubs, 12
George, William R., 18, 173
"germ theory," 9
gin-palaces, 41
girls. *See also* women
  child labor, 32, 40, 43–49, 65, 71, 78–81,
    82–83*f*
  clothing styles, 41
  in cotton industry, 79–81
  dance halls and, 41, 42, 60–61
  as "home workers," 71
  living conditions of, 32
  newspaper sales by, 65
  Progressive reforms and, viii
  prostitution and, 43–49, 146–48
  spinners, 79–80, 82–83*f*
  street work, 32, 65
  transportation for immoral purposes out-
    lawed, 174
  vocational education for, 109–10
Girl Scouts of America, 19, 174
Glaspell, Susan, 1–2

government, vii, 12–13. *See also* self-government
Great Migration, 168, 169
Great Train Robbery, The, 173
Gunckel, John, 172

half-orphans, 14, 67
Hall, G. Stanley, 173
Hamburger, Regina (Medzini), 158, 159–60
Hammer v. Dagenhart, 174
happiness, child's right to, 91–92
Harlem Renaissance, 168
Hawthorne Club playground, 93–98
health. *See also* childhood illness; child mortality
    conditions, 129–31
    of "home workers," 72–74
    middle-class concerns about, 9
    research on, 15
    in urban areas, 9–10
health care
    blindness prevention, 130–31
    for childhood illness, 97–98
    in detention homes, 118
    infant care, 15, 16, 104–6, 131–35, 172, 174
    medical inspections, 173
    mouth hygiene, 135–36
    provided by boys' organizations, 127
    for tuberculosis, 99–102
health departments, 1, 15, 103, 173
health education, 15–16, 96–98. *See also* hygiene education
    of mothers, 91, 105–6, 131, 132–35
    in self-governing recreational facilities, 96–98
    sex education, 45–46
hearing, of babies, 105
Hector, 92
Henry Street Settlement, 172
high schools
    attendance, 173, 174
    graduation rates, 22
    race relations in, 55–59
    social clubs, 58–59
    student activities, 23
    youth culture in, 22–24
Hine, Lewis, 22
    "Images of Children at Work," 81–87
Holt, Luther Emmett, 173
"home workers," 87*f*
    child labor, 8, 9
    earnings, 72, 74–76
    eyestrain in, 72, 73
    family involvement, 71, 72
    fatigue in, 73–74
    health issues, 72–74
    physical injuries, 72–74
    retardation in, 73

school attendance by, 72–73
    types of work, 71–72
    working conditions, 71–76
    working hours, 72–73
Horatio Alger, 7, 172
housework instruction, 110–11
housing conditions, 7–8, 34–35, 125, 170
How the Other Half Lives (Riis), 10, 33
"How the Other Half Lives" (Riis), 33–38
Hughes, Langston
    "Big Sea, The: An Autobiography," 168–71
Hull House, 12, 14–15, 39, 154–55, 172
hygiene education. *See also* health education
    babies, 105–6
    for "City of Hawthorne," 96–98
    of Little Mothers, 105–6

"Images from the Chicago Child Welfare Exhibit," 136–39
"Images of Children at Work" (Hine and National Child Labor Committee), 81–87
immigrant children. *See also* urban children/youth
    abandonment of, 32
    crime among, 31
    newsboys, 67–68
    school attendance by, 158, 169–70
immigrants
    adjustment of, 156–61
    Progressive response to, 3
    immorality charges, 48
income, family, children's contributions to, 68, 71, 75–76, 112, 163–64
"Industrial Home Work of Children" (United States Children's Bureau), 71–76
industrial practices
    criticism of, 76–78
    efficiency of, child labor and, 92
    machine work, 76–78
infant care, 104–6, 131–35, 172, 174. *See also* child care
    "baby tents," 15, 131–35
    baby week campaigns, 16
    bathing, 105–6, 134
    bottle feeding, 133–34
    clothing, 134
    growth and development, 104–5
    infant welfare stations, 132–35
    nursing, 133
    nutrition, 106
    rules for, 134
    sleep, 134
infant mortality, 9–10, 132, 174
infectious diseases, 1–2, 9–10, 97–98, 118, 129, 130
intelligence quotient (IQ), 174

International Council of Women, Children's Charter, 174
"Introductory Remarks" (McCormick), 124–26

"Jack Roller, The: A Delinquent Boy's Own Story" (Shaw), 149–55
Jack Roller, The: A Delinquent Boy's Own Story (Shaw), 149
"jack-rolling," 149, 153, 155
"jacks," 149
Jeter, Helen Rankin
    "Chicago Juvenile Court, The," 117–22
jewelry "home work," 72, 75
Jones Family Band, 166
"Josephine" (Baker), 161–68
journals, child welfare, 12
junior republics, 18, 173. *See also* republics
"junkers," 8–9
Juvenile Court of Chicago, 48–49, 117–22
juvenile courts, 173
    Chicago, 117–22
    detention homes, 117–22
    development of, 113–22
    establishment of, 20–21
    typical cases, 120–22
juvenile delinquency, 145–55
    automobiles and, 60
    as the "boy problem," 16–21
    burglary, 115–16, 153
    causes of, 31, 145, 149–55
    criminal behavior *vs.*, 21
    "dangerous classes" and, 30–33
    leisure time and, 11–12, 17–18
    paths to, 146–55
    recreation and, 11–12, 17–19
    reform efforts and, 16–21
    responses to, 113–22
Juvenile Protective Association, 45, 173

Keating-Owen Act of 1916, 22, 174
Kelley, Florence, 13, 88, 173
Key, Ellen, 5, 173
kindergarten, 172
Kipling, Rudyard, 92
Koch, Felix J.
    "Little Mothers of Tomorrow," 102–6
Kruesi, Walter E.
    "School of Outdoor Life for Tuberculous Children, The," 99–102

Labor Day, 158–59
labor unions, 159
lace, drawing threads on, 72, 74, 75
Lathrop, Julia C., 15, 174
laxatives, 118
League of Nations
    Declaration of the Rights of the Child, 88
leisure time. *See also* entertainment; recreation
    juvenile delinquency and, 11–12, 17–18

"Lest We Forget" *(The Newsboys' World)*, 142–43
Lindsey, Benjamin B., 20, 117
    "Dangerous Life, The," 114–17
Little Mothers
    African Americans, 103
    defined, 102
    education of, 104–6
    Little Mothers' Movement, 15, 102–6
"Little Mothers of Tomorrow" (Koch), 102–6
living conditions
    of girls, 32
    housing, 7–8, 34–35, 125, 170
    newsboys, 66–68
    in poverty, 7–8, 32, 33–38
    prostitution and, 48–49
    tenements, 34–35
    urban areas, 32–33, 34–38, 137f
local-level reforms, 3
Lodging-houses, 32
lower class
    "dangerous classes," 30–33
    Progressive attitudes toward, 6
Lower East Side, New York, 7, 34

Mabovitz, Golda (Golda Meir), 156
Mabovitz, Sheyna, 156, 157, 160
Mabovitz, Zipke, 156, 158–59
"Machines, The" (Crosby), 76–78
machine work, 76–78
Macleod, David, 26*n*.23
magazines, 61, 62, 63
magnesium sulphate, 118
Mann Act, 174
Marx, Adolph "Harpo," 24–25, 155
Marx Brothers, 24–25
Matsell, George W., 5
mayors, of self-governed recreation facilities, 94
McCormick, Cyrus H., 123, 136
    "Introductory Remarks," 124–26
medical science, 91
Meir, Golda
    "My Life," 156–61
memoirs of childhood, 155–71
    Baker, Josephine, 161–68
    Hughes, Langston, 168–71
    Meir, Golda, 156–61
messengers, 86f
middle class
    child labor and, 79
    defined, 6
    growth of, 6
middle class values
    "child-nurture" philosophy and, 6
    children's health issues and, 9–10, 15–16
    children's organizations and, 19
    child welfare reform and, 6
    youth culture and, 25

military button work, 72, 74
milk, for babies, 10
milk poisoning, 91
millinery instruction, 109
Milwaukee, 156–59
Milwaukee Normal School, 156
Milwaukee Republic, 140, 143–44
moral character, 60–63
moral indignation, 4–5
mothers. *See also* Little Mothers
  health care education of, 91, 105–6, 131, 132–35
  need for education of, 91
mouth hygiene, 135–36. *See also* dental care
moving pictures, 173
muckrakers, 76
music, 162, 163
"My Life" (Meir), 156–61

National Association for the Advancement of Colored People (NAACP), 39, 93
National Child Labor Committee (NCLC), 12, 21–22, 63, 64–70, 92, 173
  "Images of Children at Work," 81–87
National Conference on Charities and Corrections, 12
National Congress of Mothers, 12
National Consumers League, 21
nationalities
  of basket sellers, 69
  of errand boys and girls, 69–70
  of fruit venders, 68–69
  of newsboys, 66*t*
national reforms, 3
NCLC. *See* National Child Labor Committee (NCLC)
"Negro in Chicago, The: A Study of Race Relations and a Race Riot" (Chicago Commission on Race Relations), 49–59
newsboys, 8, 85*f*
  ages of, 66*t*, 67
  badges, 66
  bullies and, 65–66
  character of, 141–45
  domestic conditions of, 66–68
  earnings, 65
  essay competitions, 143–45
  girls as, 65
  immigrant children as, 67–68
  immoral influences on, 44–45
  nationalities of, 66*t*
  orphans and half-orphans, 67
  research on, 11
  salesmanship, 143–45
  school attendance, 64, 67
  views on, 140–45
  working conditions, 64–68
  working hours, 65

newsboys' associations, 64, 172
Newsboys' Protective Association, 64
newsboys' republics, 18, 140
  Milwaukee, 140, 142–43
  rules for, 140
Newsboys' World, The, 140
  essay competitions, 143–45
  "Lest We Forget," 142–43
  "Stick!" 141
  "What Is Required of the Ideal Successful Newsboy?" 143–45
newspapers
  boys' problems and, 62–63
  competition among, 65–66
New York
  Child Welfare Exhibit, 174
  Department of Health, 172
  East Side tenements, 7, 34
  Health Department, 173
  housing, 7–8, 34
  playground movement, 17
  population density, 7
  school lunches, 174
New York Charity Organization Society (COS), 12, 93
New York Society for the Prevention of Cruelty to Children, 172
Niskenkorn, Carl, 143–44
nursing, of infants, 133
nutrition
  of infants, 106, 133
  for tuberculous children, 101–2

orphans, 14, 174
  half-orphans, 14, 67
  newsboys, 67
"orphan trains," 14
"other half," 10
outdoor programs
  for tuberculous children, 99–102, 173
  for urban boys, 127–28
Outdoor Recreation League, New York City, 17
"outdoor relief," 14

"*panem et circenses*" ("bread and circuses"), 31
Parent Teacher Association, 12
penny arcades, 62
pensions, for widows, 174
Pentler, Robert, 144
Perkins, Lucy Fitch, 139
Pestalozzi, Johann, 91
Peters, William H., 103
Philadelphia, playground movement, 17
philanthropy, 123, 124
photographic documentation
  Chicago Child Welfare Exhibit, 136–38
  child labor, 81–87
physical injuries, of "home workers," 72–74
"play congresses," 17

Playground, The, 12
Playground Association of America, 12, 17, 173
playground movement, 17
playgrounds. *See also* recreation
  behavior on, 112
  children's use of, 26*n*.23
  promotion of, 12, 17
  race relations on, 53
  safety guides for, 174
"pleasure clubs," 42
pool halls, 62
"poor children's days," 13
Poplawski, Edward, 145
posters, Chicago Child Welfare Exhibit, 136–39
poverty. *See also* urban areas; urban children/youth
  child welfare and, 10–13, 33–38
  health issues and, 15–16
  living conditions in, 7–8, 32, 33–38
Progressive Era
  characteristics of, 3–5
  duration of, vii, 2
  impacts of, vii
  reforms, 2–3
  scientific research and, 2–3
prostitution
  in African American communities, 46–47
  causes of, 146–48
  children of prostitutes, 49
  conditions encouraging, 43–49
  living conditions and, 48–49
  penny arcades and, 62
  racial prejudice and, 47
  sex education and, 45–46
  study of, 43–49

race degeneracy, 92
race relations, 49–59
  community schools and, 107
  in elementary schools, 49–55
  in high schools, 55–59
  on playgrounds, 53
  social activities, 57–59
  social contacts, 54–55
  among teachers, 52
  voluntary grouping, 54, 56
race riots, 49
racial prejudice
  prostitution and, 47
  in school orchestras, 55, 57–58
  social class and, 49
Reading-rooms, 32
rebbetzin (bluestocking), 158
recreation. *See also* entertainment; playgrounds
  Boys Clubs and, 18
  facility self-government, 93–98
  juvenile delinquency and, 11–12, 17–19

  need for, 40, 41, 45
  research on, 11–12
  safety guides for, 174
  supervised facilities, 93
  for tuberculous children, 101
reformatories, 35
religion, 4
republics
  Boys' Brotherhood Republic, 18
  Ford Republic, 18
  "Junior Republic," 18
  junior republics, 173
  newsboys', 18, 140, 142–43
research. *See also* child welfare studies
  on child labor, 11, 63–87
  on children's health issues, 15–16
  on child welfare, 11–13, 43–63
  on newsboys, 11
  on prostitution, 43–49
  on recreation, 11–12
  scientific, 2–3, 173
retardation, in "home workers," 73
"right to childhood," 13
"Right View of the Child, The" (Devine), 89–93
Riis, Jacob, 10, 76, 172, 173
  "How the Other Half Lives," 33–38
"road houses," 60
robberies, 149
Robinson, Lilian V.
  "City of Hawthorne, The," 93–98
"rolling," 149
Roosevelt, Franklin, 175
Roosevelt, Theodore, 2, 4, 13
rosary bead assembly, 74, 75
Rotary Club of Los Angeles, 59
runaways, 153–55
rural living, 4, 8
Russell, Bob, 166, 167
Russell Sage Foundation, 48

Safety Institute of America, 174
salesmanship, of newsboys, 143–45
savings banks, in school, 112
school attendance
  by African Americans, 169–70
  by basket sellers, 69
  by children in detention homes, 119
  by errand boys and girls, 70
  high school, 173, 174
  by "home workers," 72–73
  by immigrant children, 158, 169–70
  by newsboys, 64, 67
School of Outdoor Life for Tuberculous Children, Boston, 99–102
"School of Outdoor Life for Tuberculous Children, The" (Kruesi), 99–102
school orchestras, racial prejudice in, 55, 57–58

schools, 106–14. *See also* education; health education; vocational education
  as community centers, 113
  health care, 173
  lunches, 174
  race relations in, 49–59
  as settlement houses, 107–14
  social responsibilities of, 106–14
  textbooks, 159–60
"Schools of Tomorrow" (Dewey and Dewey), 107–14
scientific research, 2–3, 173. *See also* research
scouting movement, 19. *See also* Boy Scouts of America; Girl Scouts of America
self-government
  children's and youth's institutions, 18–19
  discipline and, 95–96
  laws of, 94–95
  newsboys' republics, 140
  recreation facilities, 93–98
settlement houses, 12, 14–15, 17, 154–55, 172
  assistance offered by, 39
  schools as, 107–14
sewing instruction, 109, 111
sex education, 45–46
sexual abuse, 48–49
sexual behavior, 48–49
sexual intercourse, age of consent, 17
sexual perversion, 47
Shaw, Clifford R., 145
  "Jack-Roller, The: A Delinquent Boy's Own Story," 149–55
Sheppard-Towner Act, 15, 174
shoe lace packaging, 75–76
shoe-repairing instruction, 110
Shortridge High School, Indianapolis, 23
show business, 164–68
sleep, for infants, 134
small town nostalgia, 4
smoking, 61
"smutty magazines," 63
social activities, school, 57–59, 112–13
social class
  "dangerous classes," 30–33
  lower class, 6, 30–33
  middle class, 6, 9–10, 15–16, 19, 25, 79
  race relations and, 49
  upper class, 6, 92–93
  working class, 6, 8–9
social contact, between races, 54–55
"social disorganization" theory, 145
"Social Evil in Chicago, The: Study of Existing Conditions with Recommendations" (Vice Commission of the City of Chicago), 43–49, 146
Social Gospel movement, 4
Social Investigation Dept., Chicago School of Civics and Philanthropy, 48

socialism, 159
social responsibilities
  of schools, 106–14
  of students, 111–12
Society for the Prevention of Cruelty to Children, 14, 38, 172
Some Ethical Gains through Legislation (Kelley), 173
speech, of babies, 105
spinners, 79–80, 82–83*f*
"Spirit of Youth and the City Streets, The" (Addams), 39–43
spoiled children, 92–93
St. Louis, African American childhood in, 161–68
Starr, Ellen Gates, 14, 39, 172
state-level reforms, 3
"State of Columbia," 18
sterilization, 90
"Stick!" *(The Newsboys' World)*, 141
stone setting, 74, 75
"Story of My Cotton Dress, The" *(Child Labor Bulletin)*, 79–81
Street-Land: Its Little People and Big Problems (Davis), 4
street trades. *See also* basket sellers; errand boys and girls; fruit venders; newsboys
  child labor, 8–9, 32
  immoral influences, 44–45
  working conditions, 64–70
stringing tags, 72
summer jobs, 160–61
Sunday Meetings, 32

tailoring instruction, 110
"Tantine's Story" (Vice Commission of the City of Chicago), 146–48
Taylor, Canon, 37
teachers
  African American, 52–53
  race relations among, 52
  roles of, 161
"Team Work for City Boys" (Chicago Child Welfare Exhibit), 126–28
teeth, care of, 105, 135–36
tenements, 7–8
  Chicago, 170
  effects of, 125
  living conditions, 34–35
Terman, Lewis, 174
textbook fundraising campaign, 159–60
thread drawing on lace, 72, 74, 75
Tidwell, John, 84*f*
Toledo Newsboys' Association, 172
towel making, 96–97
trade schools, 35
trade unions, 159
traffic accident deaths, 8, 174
truancy, 153
tuberculosis, 99–102, 173

Uncle Tom's Cabin, 159
underwear finishing, 72
United States Children's Bureau, 15, 91,
    117, 174
    "Industrial Home Work of Children,"
    71–76
United States of Tacoma, 18
upper class, 6, 92–93
urban areas
    health concerns, 9–10
    housing conditions, 7–8, 34–35, 125,
    170
    juvenile delinquency causes, 145
    living conditions, 32–33, 34–38, 137*f*
    race relations in, 49
urban children/youth. *See also* immigrant
        children
    abandonment of, 32, 40–43
    attitudes toward, 29
    automobiles and, 59–60
    burglary, 115–16, 153, 155
    child labor, 8–9
    contribution to family income by, 68, 71,
        75–76, 112, 163–64
    crime, 30–33
    dance halls and, 61–62
    deaths of, 34
    hopes for, 124–26
    juvenile delinquency, 113–22
    magazines and newspapers and, 62–63
    moral development, 11
    recreation, 40, 41, 45
    sexual abuse, 48–49
    sexual behavior, 48–49
    spirit of, 39–43
    studies of, 43
    unhappy childhoods, 149–55
    youth culture, 22–25
U.S. Census Bureau, 9
U.S. Department of Commerce and Labor,
    8–9
    Children's Bureau, 15, 91, 117, 174

Valentino, Rudolph, 60*n*
vaudeville, 164–68
Vice Commission of the City of Chicago
    "Social Evil in Chicago, The: Study of
        Existing Conditions with Recommen-
        dations," 43–49
    "Tantine's Story," 146–48
vision. *See* eyesight

vocational education
    for boys, 110
    child's right to, 92
    in community schools, 109–11
    for girls, 109–10

Wald, Lillian, 172, 173
Washington, Booker T., 23
Western Union messengers, 86*f*
"What Is Required of the Ideal Successful
    Newsboy?" *(The Newsboys' World),*
    143–45
White House Conference on Child Welfare
    Standards, 174
White House Conference on Dependent
    Children, 12–13
"white plague," 99. *See also* tuberculosis
widows, pensions for, 174
Wiebe, Robert H., 3
Wilson, Woodrow, 2, 174
Wisconsin Home and Farm School, 19–20
Woman's Christian Temperance Union, 17
women. *See also* girls
    child welfare and, 15
    prostitution study, 43–49
women's clubs, 17
working class
    child labor in, 8–9
    Progressive attitudes toward, 6
    as victims, 6
working conditions
    basket sellers, 69
    doffer boys, 80
    errand boys and girls, 69–70
    fruit venders, 68–69
    "home workers," 71–76
    machine work, 76–78
    newsboys, 64–68
    spinners, 79–80
    "street trades," 64–70
working hours
    errand boys and girls, 70
    fruit venders, 69
    "home workers," 72–73
    newsboys, 65
Work with Boys, 12

Young Men's Christian Association
    (Y.M.C.A.), 127
youth culture, 22–25
Youth's Companion, 7